SOFT POWER SKILLS, WOMEN AND NEGOTIATIONS

By

Ida Greene, Ph.D.

© 1991, 2004 by Ida Greene, Ph.D. All rights reserved.

No part of this book may be reproduced, stored in a retrieval system, or transmitted by any means, electronic, mechanical, photocopying, recording, or otherwise, without written permission from the author.

ISBN: 1-4033-6900-3 (e-book)
ISBN: 1-4033-6901-1 (Paperback)

This book is printed on acid free paper.

1stBooks - rev. 01/19/04

TODAY'S WOMAN NEEDS TO FALL BACK ON MORE THAN
BRAINS, BRAWN AND BEAUTY

SHE NEEDS TO NEGOTIATE
As Males Have Done for Centuries
Compromise from integrity to reach an equitable
and fair solution that benefits both you and the other party.

This Book Is Dedicated to the Women and Men, Who Want to Employ Soft-Powers Skills to Get What They Want In Life.

Acknowledgments

I am indebted to my father, Willie O' Neal Green, who departed this life July 8, 1979. He taught me the nuts and bolts of selling and negotiation. He was a true entrepreneur. If anything could be sold, he sold it; a master craftsman at selling. We had a very lucrative business selling snow cones from our front porch.

At age 10, he put me on a bike and off I went to sell the portions of goat given me. I had to negotiate often to get the prices of $3, $4, $5, that he had written on the outside of each package. I never received less than the amounts he asked; most times I received more because I could keep all the extra money. I refused to accept "no". If they couldn't buy, I would weigh out a portion to fit their budget. I carried my little weigh scale and goat meat in the basket on my bike. Negotiation and selling was fun. Everyone was happy, the customer, my dad, and myself.

I wish to thank my mother who taught me about humility, and her words of wisdom, "You can catch more flies with honey than you can with vinegar," is the underlying principle of soft power negotiating skills.

And I thank God for the self discipline, persistence and divine intervention with earth angels to provide me with the necessary inspiration and motivation to keep me focused on the completion of the second printing of this book.

Negotiation can be fun. We must always come from integrity, empathy, compassion, and caring concern. If we do this when we interact with others, we will be dealt with in a just manner.

Foreword from the Author

This book will serve as an overview on negotiation for some people and a review for others. It provide concise nuts and bolts information for the novice negotiator, so that you understand what occurs when you or others negotiate. Much of this information will address the negotiation process and the skills you need to be a good negotiator. "Soft Power Negotiation Skills™" goes beyond a knowledge of theoretical negotiation concepts about how to negotiate. It looks at power and the way it is perceived and used in our society.

The negotiation process is an art form that intertwines one's ego and personality style. It requires you to have knowledge about human motivation, and an intuitive awareness about your fears, passions, strengths and weaknesses. To become a skilled negotiator, it requires that you have the ability to look beyond the words you or others use, to find the hidden meaning of what is said. It is possible to find yourself or others - overreacting, under reacting, or reacting as if on automatic pilot, to a neutral word, or statement made by the opposing party. You will need to be patient with yourself and the other party and practice tolerance. For all new learning takes times to develop and that the learning curve is not a down stroll. The curve of learning has an upward peak, down ward peak, and many flat plateaus, when no new learning is occurring.

The book will address Maslow's theory of needs, how they motivate and move us forward in our negotiations with others. It also looks at Soft Power principles, tactics and the Soft Power words.

Every negotiation we encounter will be different, because the people are different. Skill at Negotiation requires you to handle each situations with few preconceived notions about what your opponent will do. As you explore the relationship between understanding your needs, the needs of others, getting your needs met, while using Soft Power™, you will discover the basic facts that underlie all negotiation, and the principles of negotiation. The negotiation guidelines will serve as a map to point you in the right direction. To enhance your negotiation skills, learn how to identify the medium of exchange, and other influencing factors, of verbal and non-verbal expression. You will need to learn the rules of negotiation and the steps to follow. You will be able to identify and employ the three stages of negotiation in a mock work environment if you complete all the exercises. The work book components serve as a training resource as you practice mentally and verbally in the sanctuary of your home.

I encourage you to take the risks required to gain the wisdom and knowledge to negotiate softly. The negotiation process is a continuous learning experience. It requires you understand your actions and reactions, to help you better understand the behavior of others. You will find the book informative with simple steps to follow. I would love feedback about how you were able to integrate soft power negotiation skills into your present negotiation style. Please forward all comments or questions to PSI Publishers c/o Dr. Ida Greene 2910 Baily Avenue, San Diego, CA 92105-4585, 619 262-9951

Contents

CHAPTER 1 Negotiation, The Mystery Unveiled 1
CHAPTER 2 Relationship Between Getting Our Needs Met And Negotiation 5
CHAPTER 3 The Soft Side Of Power 17
CHAPTER 4 Hard Power And Stress Management 25
CHAPTER 5 Soft Power Negotiation Skills™ 35
CHAPTER 6 Non Assertion Is Not Soft Power 47
CHAPTER 7 How To Successfully Negotiate Anything 53
CHAPTER 8 The Five Negotiation Styles 63
CHAPTER 9 Manage Conflict And Anger To Move Through Negotiation 67
CHAPTER 10 Use Soft Power To Resolve Conflict 71
Soft Power Negotiation Skills 71
CHAPTER 11 Identify Your Negotiation Style To Recognize And Respond To The Style Of Others 83
CHAPTER 12 Blocks To Developing Soft Power Skills 95
CHAPTER 13 Use Positive Assertion To Enhance Your Negotiation Style 109
Index 121
Bibliography 123
About The Author 125

Chapter 1

NEGOTIATION, THE MYSTERY UNVEILED

Negotiation Is:
"A cooperative process of which no single move of one participant has the total meaning. No matter what choice you make everyone's strategy is dependent on the other person."

"Negotiation calls for the handling of situations with as few self structured barriers as possible."

"It is reason and emotion, head and heart; it is a successful blend between the heart and the mind."

"We become successful at negotiation, if we attempt to grasp the whole rather than become engrossed in detail."

"We use and make every mistake we can to gain wisdom, negotiation is a learning process."

"Life is an ever changing process. We can't expect the same results from the same actions all the time. It is trial and error."

"It is a method to arrive at a solution, where the answer does not come from within us, nor from outside of us. It is both."

"Negotiation is both an art and a game to be enjoyed, for all situations, circumstances, or people can change in an instant."

I agree with all of the above definitions. However, I find the latter definition allows for divine intervention. Sometimes when things are not going as we had hoped or planned, and we have done all we know to do, we have to let go of our human will. When we let go, we call upon a higher power to take over. Then we need to affirm or pray for divine justice and right action for all parties. Negotiation is so much a part of our daily lives that we interact/negotiate without thinking about it and set up **win/lose** experiences rather than **win/win**. The basis of all negotiation is communication, human interaction, and relationship building. The negotiation process, like people is elusive and intriguing. Just when you think you have things under control, the players, circumstances, and events shift. *Successful negotiation is the art of arriving at an agreement, that please both you and the other person.* It requires you understand your actions, and reactions to respond appropriately to the reaction of others.

I will be interchanging the word *human interaction* with the word *negotiation* through out the book. Everything we do involves negotiation. We continually trade or make concessions in life to have the things that give us pleasure or add meaning.

Negotiation occurs any time we attempt to influence the behavior of another person, to cause them to comply with our wishes and desires. It implies that a desire demands satisfaction or a need is unfulfilled. It involves the modification of a relationship through *human interaction* to reach an agreement. *Negotiation takes place whenever one person wants or needs something and the other person fulfills the need.*

We negotiate for many reasons. Some of them are listed below.

WHY WE NEGOTIATE

1. A need is unmet.
2. A desire is unfulfilled.
3. A difference of opinion exists.
4. The issue or item is negotiable—*things, positions and situation can be negotiated*, not feelings.
5. One or both parties is seeking to influence or change behavior through compromise.

Maslow has listed seven categories of needs as basic motivators of human behavior in a successive, hierarchical pattern they are:

1. Physiological needs (homeostatic—hunger, sex, warmth)

2. Safety and security needs, (job security, money in bank, home dwelling)
3. Love and belonging needs
4. Esteem needs (reputation, prestige, status, domination and the approval) of others
5. Need for self-actualization (to become what one is capable of becoming)
6. Need to know and to understand
7. Esthetics needs (order, balance, beauty)

According to Maslow, the satisfaction of our needs motivate everything we do. Since none of our needs are 100% satisfied, we are continually driven to satisfy them. If Maslow's theory is true, we may be unaware of our innate tendency to put our concerns before that of others.

Which of the above needs do you feel would be a factor in your negotiation/interactional deliberations?

Why is this need important in your life at this time?

Ida Greene, Ph.D.

WHAT'S YOUR BEHAVIORAL STYLE?

DIRECTOR	SOCIALIZER	RELATOR	THINKER
DOMINANCE	EMOTIONAL	STEADY	PERFECTIONIST
DOER	EXPRESSIVE	STABLE	COMPLIANT
LEADER	DISORGANIZED	LOYAL	COMPETENT
EGO ORIENTED	INSPIRATIONAL	LISTENER	PROBLEM SOLVER
OPINIONATED	PERSUADER	LIKES STATUS QUO	FACTS
CREATIVE	SPONTANEOUS	PATIENT	RULES
DIRECT	PLAYFUL	WARM	CAUTIOUS
COMPETITIVE	ENTHUSIASTIC	FRIENDLY	ACCURATE
AGGRESSIVE	INTERACTIVE	SUPPORTIVE	DETAILED
DECISIVE	TRUSTING	AMICABLE	ANALYTICAL
BUSINESSLIKE	OPTIMISTIC	PREDICTABLE	HIGH STANDARDS
DRIVING	CHARMING	COMPLACENT	DATA
DEMANDING	MOTIVATOR	SINCERE	CORRECT
BLUNT	FASHIONABLE	TEAM PLAYER	PLANNER

Check only words that MOST represent your behavioral style

TREAT PEOPLE THE WAY THEY WANT TO BE TREATED

Sandra Schrif

Chapter 2

RELATIONSHIP BETWEEN GETTING OUR NEEDS MET AND NEGOTIATION

Negotiation is a part of our life. We negotiate for things on a daily basis. However, we rarely get what we want, and we are left feeling dejected and unfulfilled. Successful negotiation requires planning and a thorough knowledge of what the other person wants or desires. To be successful in any negotiation you and the other person must have a shared goal. There must be a commonality of need or desire for the other party to hear what you have to offer. You must first, take time to find out if what you have to offer is what the other person wants or desires. You must understand your needs and those of the other person.

Negotiation requires that you have good listening skills, and people skills. *The ability to not talk (listen), will enable you to extract information from others.* It is a skill worth learning if you desire success as a negotiator. Because the strength of your desire to negotiate to get what you want will be based on your need at the time. First know what you desire, or would like to have. Write your answer to the questions listed below. You may use an extra sheet of paper if needed.

1. What do you desire today, to have or get?
2. How much risk are you willing to take, to get what you desire?
3. Is there a negative outcome or draw back to having what you desire at this time? What is it?

No two people will ever want the same thing. So before you attempt to negotiate or bargain with a person, find out what they want. Then find a way to give them what they want. This will make them happy and create a desire in them to return the favor. First identify the medium of exchange in a negotiation (money, time, commodity), to see if you have what the other party wants.

Once you have decided to have a cooperative negotiation exchange, and you know what your opponent wants, begin to set the stage to have a win/win communication exchange. When you make the decision before you start your negotiation proceedings you are less likely to sabotage your goals. Often we negotiate with a hidden agenda, or an ulterior motive due to our expectation of a negative outcome from prior conditioning. And we may be unaware of our bias, or blind spot. You may also withhold information, demonstrate a lack of trust, or confidence in yourself or your ability to barter. Everything we do has meaning.

All of our behavior is conscious or unconscious. Conscious means you have knowledge of your behavior and you are aware of what you say or do. This behavior is called an emotion. Our emotions are highly charged because they have some of the negative imprints of our parents or childhood caretakers. Our feelings are more transient and fleeting. They are not as deeply ingrained as our emotions and they are more under our volition and control. We can be positively or negatively affected by the emotions others express and likewise others are affected by the negative emotions we display when they are in our presence.

All of our feelings and emotional expressions are filed and stored in our subconscious mind. They are easily retrieved with a stimulus like the original stimulus. This is why we do not need to figure out how to respond in a given situation and why we act or react instantly.

The word subconscious or unconscious means you lack mental awareness of your actions and reactions. They are stored in the computer of your mind and hidden from your awareness. The subconscious mind is always active. It never goes to sleep. It acts as a driver of our emotions and feelings and determines how we will act or react. Our unconscious mind knows only how to react. It does this without our conscious awareness, so that we respond appropriately. Listed below are some unconscious drives and conscious feelings that interplay when you interact with others. They act like a hidden agenda in our interactions with others.

Unconscious Motivators of Behavior are:

1. Repression - Convenient forgetting of an unpleasant past event or future event.

2. Displacement - Taking out our anger and aggression on persons or objects that are not the cause of our difficulty.

3. Rationalization - To interpret things or situations in a manner that will place us in a favorable light. To justify our behavior.
4. Projection - To attribute your motives to another person. (i.e to accuse someone of being money hungry, when it is you).

Can you identify unconscious drives that may influence the way you negotiate? What are they? Write them down now.

Conscious Motivators of Behavior

Feelings present during negotiation are:

1. Revenge, wounded pride etc.
2. Need to outdo others, be "top dog."
3. Jealousy (wanting to do what another is doing or wanting what another has).
4. Greed

Write down any feelings listed above, that may influence whether you negotiate (barter) or decide the way you negotiate.

To better understand the negotiation process, you must be aware of all factors that may influence the outcome of your interaction with the person you want to comply with your desire. The factors involved in all negotiation are:

1. Communication: Listening and acting based on what we hear.

2. Relationship: Open/closed. An open relationship is with a family member, friend or significant other (husband, wife, child); here you are likely to be friendly and less guarded since a foundation of trust has been established. A closed relationship is one where you have minimal personal information about the person; so you need to establish rapport first and then go through the steps of building a relationship through trust, caring, compassion, understanding, and tolerance.

3. Attitude: Positive/negative. We feel closer to those people or things we hold in a positive frame of reference and repelled by those things or persons we view negatively.

4. Creativity: The decision to create your life from choice as opposed to being a reactionary person. What is your pattern? How can you create what you desire. Write your answer below.

5. Self-Image: The right to have one's needs and basic desires met. It is the image you hold of yourself. <u>Is it one of competence or incompetence?</u>

6. Self-Esteem: Self-worth and self-deserving. Your worth as a person. Do you see yourself as important in the total scheme of life? In what way?

    a. Do you know why you were created?

    b. Do you have a compelling reason for being alive?

    If you can not resoundingly say yes without hesitation, I recommend you get both the book on Self-Esteem and the audio cassette tape album on "Light the Fire Within You."

7. Self-Confidence: Self-Assurance and the ability to act and behave according to one's belief. The courage to speak or act in your behalf when others belittle you or make disparaging

remarks about you; when the comments are/were untrue. The objective under these circumstances is not to react defensively but to come to your defense when needed. At times the wisest thing to do when criticized is to silently defend yourself in your mind, especially if you are in a public gathering and it would be improper to do otherwise at the time.

8. Orientation to life: the way you problem solve and resolve conflict, your life pattern. Do you look at ways to amicably resolve conflict with others or do you see life as a battle ground where there is no retreat or corrections allowed. Do you handle disagreements through reasoning, arguing, overpowering, threats, or intimidation? Write down how you usually respond.

9. Cultural orientation may dictate how you handle contracts or business matters ex. The Oriental culture likes to establish a relationship and then discuss the issue. The Japanese culture likes to explore all the options before deciding on a particular idea. The Asian and Latin American culture often concur as a group/family rather than as an individual as most Anglo Saxon Americans. For African American, and American Indians, their fear level may be high and trust, low due to past acts of bias and discrimination.

   A. Write down any reflections you have right now.

   B. To get others to agree with you, create value for them to want to hear what you have to offer.

   C. Write out what you want to occur between you and the person you want to influence. Do it now.

   D. Discuss points of disagreement between you and the other person, Give them the opportunity first, to correct any misunderstanding between the two of you. After the two of you agree, state your comments or concerns.

E. For any disagreed issues in a negotiation, state what you desire, then write out your newer version of what you want, then have them sign or initial the new version.

F. Always keep foremost in mind that the negotiation process can be likened to you feeding an unpalatable food (idea) to a person. It may be hard for people to swallow (*accept*) what you want to give them.

G. Remember, an underlying mixed motive may exist and may be seen by the other person as trickery or manipulation. What did you learn from this section? Write down your comments now.

10. Life Position: Our life position is a reflection of how we see ourself in relation to others. it may be: powerful/powerless, control/no control, independent/ dependent, choice/no choice. How do you see yourself? Circle words that best describe you. Can you change or modify the circumstances in your life?

    A. Do you see yourself as having power? How do you utilize this power in your life? Explain how.

    B. Do you feel able to take care of yourself, or are you looking for someone to take care of you?

11. Cultural Background - Find out if the person is native to the customs of your culture or if they are foreign born. Even if they were born in your country, there may still be differences due to their adoption of traditional folk ways or certain ideologies.

To be a good negotiator, you need to be alert to every clue of information that can help you better understand your opponent. Know in specifics what you want, and what the other person wants so you can develop a plan to satisfy both needs. Look for any small details that can explain others' behavior.

12. Non-verbal communication (body language)

    1. Body language conveys shades of meaning through psychological overtones and undertones. You can better understand your opponent's thinking by observing his/her body language because every movement has meaning.

    A. Body posture - we lean forward when interested, and back away when disinterested.

13. Non-verbal expressions may indicate fear, anxiety, or extreme nervousness and may be shown by:

    1. Facial expression - twitching of facial muscles, eyes, quivering of the lips may indicate fear or nervousness.

    2. Behavioral mannerisms that indicate tension are: a. staring into the silence, b. undue preoccupation with objects like - papers, pens etc. c. blushing, d. cough e. laughter f. giggling g. fidgeting.

14. Personal Power - The ability to influence people to obtain things you want, or do things you want. Power can be experienced as "Hard or Soft Power." Most negotiation tactics are competitive rather than cooperative. We define this approach as hard hitting and "Hard Power". We use "Hard Power" when we bull doze through a negotiation, using force, intimidation and scare tactics to obtain our objective. In Soft Power^{TM}, you are concerned about the relationship, and how the outcome will affect the other person. You take time before you negotiate to establish rapport, trust and friendship. This helps to feel you are interacting with a trusted friend. So you are less fearful, and able to negotiate in good faith.

There are many kinds of power, they include Connection Power, Referent Power, Charismatic Power, Authoritarian/ Coercive Power, Information Power, Reward Power, and Other Power Roles:

1. Connection Power—is based on the leader's "connections" with influential or important persons inside or outside the organization. Others aim at gaining the favor or avoiding the disfavor of the powerful connection.

2. Referent Power—The person is well known or associated with a cause. (i.e. Oprah Winfrey, Mother Teresa, Bob Hope). If you used this form of power you would make an association between the character traits of this person and yourself.

3. Charismatic Power—The ability to excite others into action, through one's mystique, presence, or aura.

4. Authoritarian/Coercive Power— Getting people to do what they don't want to do through the use of fear or intimidation. It induces compliance because failure to comply might lead to punishment or displeasure. And the power vested in one's position, if one is in a position to change the lives of others. An example of this kind of power in the work force would be, firing of employees and job transfers.

5. Information Power—Knowledge you possess or can acquire through research. To use this knowledge as a leverage to control or induce fear in others.

6. Reward Power—is based on the leader's ability to provide rewards for other people. These people believe that their compliance will lead to gaining positive incentives such as pay, promotion, or recognition.

7. Other Power Roles—Dysfunctional relationship: passive aggressive, co dependent, victim/"poor me" - We give our power away in all of these roles because we are afraid, or we see ourself as unable to assume responsibility for our decisions

or behavior. Due to learned self denial, destructive addictive behavior patterns, we may act helpless, incapable, or confused. We may manipulate others, or allow ourself to be manipulated to satisfy a learned dysfunctional way of feeling cared for or about.

Which of the above forms of dysfunctional power would you identify as hard Power™ or Soft Power™. Write your answer below and state why you chose this power. ex. #4 Authoritarian Power.

The forms of power I identify as Hard Power™ are: Authoritarian, Connection, Information, or other Dysfunctional types of power. Examples of Soft Power™ are: Referent, Charismatic, and Reward. However if the reward is used to intimidate or enforce compliance it is Hard Power™. If you do not like how you feel when you interact with someone who uses Hard Power, the better choice is Soft Power™. Soft Power™ is based on positive assertion and Hard Power™ uses aggression to accomplish its tasks.

If you want to be assertive, but find you are stopping yourself with fearful thoughts about the outcome of your assertion, you need to examine your thoughts to look for irrational thinking. When we focus on the negative outcome of an assertive act before considering other options, we are thinking in an irrational manner. To be effective in the use of soft power, it will require you to replace irrational thinking with rational thinking. This will reduce your anxiety and allow you time to assess the situation.

Hard power is an outer act of aggressive behavior we use in our interactions with others. It is based on our irrational fears about ourself and life events. Most of us are acquainted with the use of "hard power" because it is woven within the matrix of our societal values. It is a by product from the pioneer settler days in the United States. The power structure then employed aggression and force to conquer land and subjects. From this structure emerged the behaviors of toughness, intimidation, aggression, force, dominance, and rulership. It was common and acceptable to attack if threatened with a loss of power or threat of bodily harm. We use "Hard Power" when we bulldoze through a negotiation using force, intimidation or scare tactics to obtain our objective. We tacitly legitimize hard power through the acknowledgement, recognition and use of force, aggression, or intimidation in our business/personal encounters. Hard power uses force verbal/mental, emotional or physical abuse and degradation to manipulate or control others.

The factors involved in hard power are:

1. Communication - two way exchange. listening and acting based on what one hear.

2. Relationships - are closed because the feelings of others are not considered important to the relationship.

3. Power - Can be negative or positive, depending upon the kind of power.

4. Life Position - Our attitude about ourself, determines how we treat ourselves and others. Powerful persons do not need to control the action or reactions of others.

5. Independent/dependent - The person using the power acts independent; the role of the recipient is dependent.

Hard Power^{TM} is characterized by the following personality types:

1. The Intimidator: Their superior attitudes and threatening actions are calculated to scare or somehow force you into agreement with them.

2. The Critic: Everything you do is wrong. Their constant harping, fault finding and "you can't do it" messages block your performance and stifles growth.

3. The Bully: They love to make you feel uncomfortable. Insecurity drives them to build their own confidence by reducing the confidence of others.

4. The Bragger: Works hard to control others through emotional ploys and personal politics, they try to avoid taking

responsibility for anything. They lead you to believe it is your fault when things go wrong.

HARD-POWER

1. Competitive, Get a "High" From Winning -
2. Dominant/Controlling -
3. Forceful/Intimidates -
4. Makes Concessions Grudgingly -
5. May Not Respect Rights/Feelings of Others -
6. Calculated and Cunning Planner (<u>Words</u> and <u>Actions</u> Differ)-
7. Feels Devastated by "No" Answer -
8. Overall Goal, "Out Beat the Competition" -

Hard Power character traits are:

- A. Tough - thinks negative, lack of compassion,
- B. Dominant - controls and rule over people.
- C. Forceful - uses coercion, and fear tactics to over power and control.
- D. Aggressive - verbally abuses, may escalate to physical abuse if frustrated or one's needs are not met.
- E. Attacks - deals harshly with others, criticizes, humiliates and condemn.
- F. Intimidates - Has a negative outlook about people; frightens and bully others.
- G. Person does not ask for what they want, tends to take what is not rightfully theirs.

Treatment For Fear

With God's help I am in control. My fears subside and the cause of them passes. They were never the truth. Fear is only a false illusion appearing as real. God's love is the truth and only power, and it is protecting me now. I have absolute peace of mind. Peace like a river is cleansing me of fear right now. A circle of Light surrounds me, and nothing of harm can enter my physical, mental, or spiritual

Ida Greene, Ph.D.

world. I am guided into right action and clear thinking. Only love goes from me and only love returns to me. Thank you, Father, Mother, God; you are all I need.

Chapter 3

THE SOFT SIDE OF POWER

Most of us equate the word *Negotiation,* with the word "men." And we also associate the word power with "men." Let's play a mental game. Close your eyes, think the word power. See what mental image runs through your mind. If you are a woman, it is unlikely that you will instantly associate the word "woman" with power or negotiation. You more than likely will think of the negative connotation of the word power and associate the word manipulative or conniving with the word woman or women. Go through this word association several times to see if the word association changes.

Because men have been the traditional providers of the family we have come to think of them as tough negotiators or persons of power, or as persons who need to feel powerful. We do not need to redefine the words negotiation and power for women. we only need to change our word associations to "people." All of nature has dominant and restorative qualities. Human beings are no different.

The dominance of the male character and the gentleness or softness of the female character, are examples of dominant and restorative traits. I refer to the gentleness of the female character, as a restorative traits and an example of soft power. Women need to realize that the character traits of females are positive, just as those of the male. We just need to make positive word associations in our mind when we think of a woman or a female.

What Is Soft Power?
Soft Power^{TM} is the understanding of the self to better know how others feel, what they want, desire, and how to meet those needs to get what you want. It is the use of soft word that support, and cooperative behaviors that enhances you in your total expression as a person. It is an ongoing process as you discover what will meet the needs of the other person, so they are willing to give you what you want. The use of soft words support your efforts and make others

want to help you. Soft words are soothing, healing, and helps foster a positive response from others.

How Does Soft Work?
It is the blending and interplay between your *personal skills and people skills* that allow others to experience you in either a positive or negative fashion defines your negotiation style.

How to Develop Soft Power
1. Start by working on your acceptance of self. You do this so you will avoid rejection of your self, and project a positive self-image. Because other people act as a mirror, and reflect back to us how we are behaving or image ourselves.

2. Self Image - When you like the image of yourself you project to others, you accept and acknowledge that you deserve to have your needs met. You are open in your communication and relations with others. And have established boundaries for yourself that you do not let others trespass, for to do so would violate your person hood and self respect. ex. you are eating a sandwich and a coworker walks up and breaks off a portion without asking. This shows a lack of concern and respect for your welfare. Because you have boundaries, you decide before hand what things you will or will not accept and you calmly let others know when they have overstepped those boundaries.

3. Work on your beliefs about what males/females can do or should do. Some stereotypical beliefs are: Males: strong, knowledgeable, to be respected, powerful and females are weak, emotional, not to be trusted, powerless

4. Attitudes - Your attitude about the following words can influence the way you think and interact with others. Write the first word that comes to mind you associate with these word:

        A. Conflict - word_____
        B. Power   - word_____
        C. Struggle - word_____
        D. Friend   - word_____

E. Foe   - word_____
F. Villain - word_____

5. Authority Figures - Your feelings about and towards authority figures can and will affect how you behave, and respond to persons who oversee your work. Words that are emotionally charged for many people, and may cause over reaction are:

A. Fear
B. Push
C. You will
D. You have to
E. This is an order
F. You need to
G. I command you
H. Now

6. Relationships - whether supportive or antagonistic can be disruptive and toxic in the ways you respond to others. Some relationships are harmonious and others are not. What could you do right now to harmonize your relationships with others?

7. Power Struggle/Tug of War - How can you change this behavioral dynamic, to be less combative and more gentle.

8. Control - Are you afraid to not be in control or in charge of things? Is your self-esteem tied to being on top, having others obey your command, or do as you say? Can you relinquish control and still feel good about yourself? If any of these are issues for you, it is in your best interest to seek professional counseling so that you are not hooked into responding in an automatic manner, and overreact to people, circumstances, or situations.

9. Communication - What is your communication pattern with your: A. Voice (Tone) B. Word Usage (formal or colloquial), Do you use the words we, you, or, us to create collaborative connections with others; or do you over use the word "I. The use of the word "I" isolates you from others.

10. People Skills - Your people skills sets the stage for how you will interact with others. If you are comfortable with and like yourself, you generally will get along with other people.

11. Self Discipline - Is the ability to master your negative and self destructive tendencies through a set of values and principles you will follow to develop emotionally and spiritually. It is gggod to be aware of your self-destructive and negative thoughts so that you self correct to be in control of your behavior rather than be controlled by an outer force. The person who can master their mind, masters their life by overcoming fear, doubt, and the "what if's," is one who can master themselves and their world. The following are emotional states you will need to improve before you see a permanent change in your behavior: A. Envy B. Fear C. Anger D. Resentment E. Hate F. Jealousy G. Revenge

To Harmonize Relationships

Do not demean, don't Challenge, don't interrupt, don't assume everyone will do what you expect, don't patronize, don't speak for others, don't think someone is exceptional, including yourself, notice what you expect from others, know that others may not always speak about the issues at hand, which you propose, respect and welcome disagreement.

Hard Power is an outward act of agressive behavior we use in our interactions with others. It is based on our irrational fears about ourself and life events. Most of us are acquainted with the use of "Hard Power," because it is woven within the matrix of our societal values. It is a by product from the pioneer settler days in the United States. The power structure then employed aggression and force to conquer land and subjects. From this structure emerged the behaviors of toughness, intimidation, aggression, force, dominance, and rulership. It was common and acceptable to attack if threatened with a loss of power or threat of bodily harm. We use "Hard Power when we bulldoze through a negotiation using force, intimidation, or scare tactics to obtain our objective. We tacitly legitimize "Hard Power"

SOFT POWER SKILLS, WOMEN AND NEGOTIATIONS

through the acknowledgement, recognition and use of force, aggression, or intimidation in our business/personal encounters. Hard Power uses force, verbal/ mental, emotional or physical abuse and degradation to manipulate or control others.

The Factors involved in Hard Power are:

1. Communication - One way communication. Listening and acting based on what one hear.

2. Relationships - Are closed because the feelings of others are not considered important to the relationship.

3. Attitude - Is negative most of the time.

4. Life Position - Our attitude about ourself, determines how we treat ourselves and others. Powerful persons do not need to control the actions or reactionms of others.

5. Independent/dependent - The person using the power acts independent. The role of the recipient is dependent.

6. Orientation to life - The way you problem solve and resolve conflict. you see others as a problem, and life as a power struggle.

The factors involved in hard power are:

1. Communication - two way exchange, listening and acting based on what one hears.

2. Relationships - are closed because the feelings of others are not considered important to the relationship.

3. Power - Can be negative or positive, depending upon the kind of power.

4. Life Position - Our attitude about ourself, determines how we treat ourselves and others. Powerful persons do not need to control the action or reactions of others.

5. Independent/dependent - The person using the power acts independent; the role of the recipient is dependent.

Hard Power™ is characterized by the following personality types:

1. The Intimidator: Their superior attitudes and threatening actions are calculated to scare or somehow force you into agreement with them.

2. The Critic: Everything you do is wrong. Their constant harping, fault finding and "you can't do it" messages block your performance and stifle growth.

3. The Bully: They love to make you feel uncomfortable. Insecurity drives them to build their own confidence by reducing the confidence of others.

4. The Bragger: Works hard to control others through emotional ploys and personal politics, they try to avoid taking responsibility for anything. They lead you to believe it is your fault when things go wrong.

HARD-POWER

1. Competitive, Get a "High" From Winning
2. Dominant/Controlling
3. Forceful/Intimidates
4. Makes Concessions Grudgingly
5. May Not Respect Rights/Feelings of Others
6. Calculated and Cunning Planner (<u>Words</u> and <u>Actions</u> Differ)
7. Feels Devastated by "No" Answer
8. Overall Goal is to, "Out Beat The Competition"

Hard Power character traits are:

A. Tough - thinks negative, lack of compassion, B. Dominant - controls and rule over people. C. Forceful - uses coercion, and fear tactics to over power and control. D. Aggressive - verbally abuses, may escalate to physical abuse if frustrated or one's needs are not met. E. Attacks - deals harshly with others, criticizes, humiliates and condemn. F. Intimidates - has a negative outlook about people; frightens and bully others. G. Person does not ask for what they want, tends to take what is not rightfully theirs.

AFFIRMATION TO DEVELOP SOFT POWER SKILLS

I give thanks for the beauty of the earth, for the trees and for the skies, and for all life. I give thanks for the nurturing qualities of love, peace, warmth, and gentleness present in me. Today I resolve anew to live in harmony with my earthly environment and to love and respect every living thing.

Ida Greene, Ph.D.

Chapter 4

HARD POWER AND STRESS MANAGEMENT

Strong negative emotions in your conscious and subconscious mind take a great toll on your body: physically, emotionally, and mentally. The emotions of resentment, anger, hate, and jealously, all interfere with the normal physiological functions in your body. The science of Psycho-Neuro-Endocrin- ology has confirmed these facts.

When you resent or hate somebody, you are the one that bears the effect of these emotions on your body. These emotions disrupt your body's normal functions and can cause or contribute to the development of disease processes such as heart disease, cancer, high blood pressure, ulcers and other physiological ailments.

Emotions which originated years ago are stored in your conscious and subconscious mind. They interfere with your body functions, your emotional and mental well-being.

The use of forgiveness affirmations is a simple way to let go, to release negative emotions from the mind. The process is very easy and powerful. It will work for you whether you believe it or not. Do this exercise daily for a month and you will see wonderful results.

Do your affirmations in the following manner - Visualize or think of the person you are angry with. It may be a person, group of people, organization, or any one from your past or present. Include yourself in this process if you feel guilty or sorry for things you have done. Mentally declare to yourself "I fully and freely forgive you, I let you go to your good quickly and in peace. All things between us has been resolved with peace and harmony for all concerned. I do this with peace in my heart."

It is also important to ask for forgiveness from people you have hurt intentionally or unintentionally. To do this, visualize yourself or think of whoever you need to ask to forgive you. Mentally declare as if speaking to them: "You fully and freely forgive me. You loose me and let me go to my good quickly and in peace. All things between us has been resolved with peace, love and harmony for all concerned.

Remember, to do these affirmations mentally in your mind. Do them regularly several times a day for a few minutes, preferably when you are in a relaxed state or when somebody arouses anger in you. Do it with everybody you have difficulty with in your life.

To see everyone as perfect, including yourself, will improve everything in your life.

POWER

Unless you choose to do great things with it,
it makes no difference how much you are rewarded,
or how much power you have.

-Oprah Winfrey

The Physiology of Stress

You have a central nervous system with two major branches. One of the branches, your "arousal network", is called the Sympathetic Nervous System. Whenever we interpret a situation as threatening, the sympathetic nervous system is activated instantaneously. Once activated, it charges the body with a powerful family of hormones. Each hormone in the family plays a specific role in mobilizing the body to meet the threat. Cortisol increases blood sugar and speeds up the body's metabolism, epinephrine helps supply extra glucose to serve as fuel for the muscles and norepinephrine also speeds up heart beat and blood pressure to fuel the muscles. I will collectively refer to this family as the stress response.

Next, I want to introduce the concept of an episode. A threatening event triggered a natural sequence of additional events resulting in a complete episode. For this episode, there were three key events;

1) the stressor, or Saber-Toothed Tiger,

2) the stress response, or interpretation and release of stress hormones, and

3) the fight, or flight response.

Whenever you perceive an event as threatening whether it is real or imagined, a sequence of events occur inside the body to create an episodic event. The <u>first</u> event is the threatening stressor (real or imagined). <u>Next</u> occurs the stress response, or interpretation and release of stress hormones. The <u>third</u> event to occur is the fight or flight response within the body.

Now you either defend yourself or flee to safety. We are socialized not to physical fight so we escape into our minds and mentally tell the body everything is O.K. When it is not O.K. So the Sympathetic Nervous System releases the extra hormones inside the body, we get a physiological rushing sensation which generates a bodily coping mechanism, that it is unique to our body (uniquely our own). People have been observed to display the following bodily reactions: eye flutter or twitch, clenched teeth or biting inside the mouth, quiver of the mouth, eye or any muscle in the body, shrugging or moving the shoulder muscles, tightening the neck muscles, clenching the fingers or hands to create white knuckles, tightening of the abdominal muscles, shakiness of the knees or entire body and you may have created a bodily response to a stressor that is uniquely your own. If it is not listed, please add it to the list.

After you respond in one of the above ways, the stress hormones are expended and you return to a balanced condition called homeostasis.

In the words of Dr. Hans Selye, the father of stress research, "Life is no longer an episode." We invariable halt the process after the stress response, and unknowingly block the natural sequence of hormone elimination through rigorous physical activity. Modern life rarely offers the luxury of jogging for twenty minutes every time we find ourselves angry or upset.

Few people are aware of how often they activate the stress response on a day-to-day basis and even fewer are consciously aware of the specific events that repeatedly cause them to be stressed. The end result and major problem is an accumulation of stress hormones brought about by a world that has simply become too busy, too crowded, and too complex.

Because stress significantly alters the body's hormonal balance, we can accurately conclude that a price is paid for the resulting accumulation of stress hormones is the debilitating effect on the immune system. Researchers have found that the body's production of cancer fighting cells, including T-lymphocytes and macrophage is reduced by the presence of stress hormones. The observation that most of us will experience a cold or flu symptoms after a bout with stress is a manifestation of the suppressed immune system.

Too many activations without elimination create and sustain a hormonal imbalance that has both short term and long term effects in determining our general health and the quality of our lives.

First, we are producing too many stress hormones, so we have to work at decreasing our production. Improve our defense or mechanism. Second, the accumulation of stress hormones suppresses the immune system and elevates our cholesterol levels, so we need to incorporate into our lifestyles activities that will eliminate the stress hormones on a regular basis and keep our body in good physical condition.

Decreasing Production

Not every stress event need to create a stress response. The key is mental discipline. Slow elevators, long lines, burnt toast how many of our stress responses are triggered by events that have no physical solutions? The culprit is you and your personality. As we pass through this life's experience we collect habits. Some of them serve us well and others need to be modified or deleted from our personality.

At the end of each day, ask yourself, how many times did I activated my sympathetic nervous system today? And to the best of your recollection, attempt to recall the specifics of the incident that caused you to feel a negative emotion. The goal is to reduce your production of stress hormones and the technique can be summed up in one word — COPING. Coping is a skill you have to work at it a little bit every day. Learn to handle adversity without getting upset or angry.

The most difficult problem that will affect you is grief. Repeated and prolonged contacts with grieving people will have an effect on you. The very nature of your responsibilities to the sick and injured prevents you from showing your true emotions; the "calm and professional manner" that you must maintain when you are handling a crisis prevents you from letting your own emotions of grief and sorrow show.

You are vulnerable to all the stresses that go with your profession. You must learn to recognize the symptoms of stress so that it does not interfere with your work or life away from work, including your family life. The signs and symptoms of chronic stress may not be obvious at first; they may be subtle and not present all of the time. The following may indicate a delayed grief reaction or the presence of excessive stress:

- An increase in stress-related physical complaints: headaches, gastrointestinal symptoms, and unexplained aches and pains.
- Anger and hostility, against your friends, the system, even patients.
- Feelings that life has lost its meaning; apathy, despair, sadness; or lack of enthusiasm.

- Feelings characteristic of depression: chronic fatigue, difficulty sleeping, lack of concentration, loss of appetite, or even bouts of uncontrollable weeping.
- Periods of intense anxiety, even panic.
- Suicidal thoughts.
- Repeated thoughts about death, suffering, or pain.
- Nightmares.
- Alcohol and substance abuse.
- Flashbacks (vivid recollections) of severe accidents, tragedies, or incidents on the job.
- Loss of interest in family and in social activities.
- Desire to quit work.

Any of these symptoms may indicate chronic stress or delayed grief.

Ida Greene, Ph.D.

BEHAVIORAL SYMPTOMS

Think about ... the past month. For each of the symptoms listed, circle how often it has occurred to you.

1. Blaming others.........................
2. Bossiness..............................
3. Irritability...........................
4. Impatience............................
5. Anger.................................
6. Inflexibility..........................
7. Drinking..............................
8. Taking aspirin and other pain relievers
9. Difficulty meeting commitments.........

Never	Once or Twice	Every Week	Nearly Every Day
0	1	2	3
0	1	2	3
0	1	2	3
0	1	2	3
0	1	2	3
0	1	2	3
0	1	2	3
0	1	2	3
0	1	2	3

___ + ___ + ___ = ___

OPTIMAL	BALANCE	STRAIN	TOTAL SCORE BURNOUT
0-3	4-6	7-9	10

SOFT POWER SKILLS, WOMEN AND NEGOTIATIONS

EMOTIONAL SYMPTOMS

Think about...the past <u>month</u>. For each of the symptoms listed, indicate how often it has occurred to you.

1. Nervous or anxiety..................
2. Worrying.............................
3. Fatigue..............................
4. Depressed..........................
5. Fearful..............................
6. Hopeless...........................
7. Forgetting important things.........
8. Crying easily.......................
9. Cannot turn off certain thoughts......

Never	Once or Twice	Every Week	Nearly Every Day
0	1	2	3
0	1	2	3
0	1	2	3
0	1	2	3
0	1	2	3
0	1	2	3
0	1	2	3
0	1	2	3
0	1	2	3
___ +	___ +	___ =	___
OPTIMAL	BALANCE	STRAIN	TOTAL SCORE BURNOUT
0-3	4-6	7-9	10

PRACTICE DEMONSTRATION IN STRESS MANAGEMENT

A simple tool for improving your skills in stress management is the relaxation and visualization process:

Sit comfortably with your spine straight. Keep your legs and hands uncrossed. Start breathing through your nose slowly and comfortable. Fill your chest and abdomen with air. Hold your breath at the end of inspiration for two or three seconds. Then, you inhale slowly and comfortably through your nose. As you inhale you let all the muscles in your body relax pleasantly and peacefully. Hold your breath for two or three seconds at the end of expiration. You do this for a few moments.

As you are getting relaxed, you visualize breathing in relaxation, peace, love and harmony as you inhale. You let this relaxation flow into your chest, heart, stomach, every part in your body and all levels of your consciousness. As you exhale, visualize blowing away any tension and disharmony stored in your body all levels of your mind. As you continue to breathe in slowly and peacefully, you get into a deeper level of relaxation, peace and harmony. As you exhale, you blow away any tension and emotion that prevents you from achieving perfect peace, balance and harmony. Repeat this process for twenty minutes daily. You can improve your physical, emotional and mental well-being by doing this process daily.

RELAXATION RESPONSE

- Sitting in hard back chair.
- Feet relaxed, and flat to the floor.
- Back straight against the chair.
- Shoulders pulled back.
- Head centered over your body.
- No parts of your body should be crossed.
- Close your eyes.
- Tell each part of your body to RELAX.
- Go through each part listed and tell it to RELAX — head, scalp, forehead, cheeks, ears, jaws, neck, shoulders, chest, arms, stomach, legs, calves, feet.

- Be in touch with this feeling of relaxation.
- Start with your head and make a wave of relaxation flow from top to bottom. Do this three times.
- Concentrate on this feeling of relaxation.
- You can obtain this feeling of relaxation any time you want by following these steps.
- Count from one to ten slowly telling your body to feel alive and awakened. Stand up slowly and stretch.

Ida Greene, Ph.D.

Chapter 5

SOFT POWER NEGOTIATION SKILLS™

Negotiation is a process which occurs any time we attempt to influence the behavior of another so as to cause them to comply with our wishes and desires. It implies that a *desire* demands satisfaction and a *need* is unfulfilled. It involves the changing of a relationship through communication to reach an agreement.

"Soft Power Negotiation™" goes beyond a knowledge of theoretical concepts about how to negotiate; it looks at power, the way it is perceived and used in our society. The negotiation process is an art form that intertwines your ego and personality style. It requires you have knowledge about human motivation, and awareness about your fears, passions, strengths and weaknesses.

To become a skilled negotiator, requires you have the ability to look beyond the words you and others use, to find the hidden meaning of what is said. Because, it is possible for you or others to over react, under react, or to react, as if on an automatic pilot, to a neutral word, or statement made by the opposing party. You will need to be patient with yourself and practice tolerance, for all new learning takes times to develop on an uphill curve of learning.

Keep in mind maslow's theory of needs, about how they motivate and move us forward in our negotiations/interactions with others. Every negotiation we encounter will be different, because the persons are different. Skill at negotiation requires you handle each situations with few preconceived notions about what your opponent will do.

None of our needs are ever 100% satisfied. Therefore we will continually strive to meet them through the negotiation process. Can you identify needs within yourself that are incomplete? List them below:

1.
2.
3.
4.

Soft Power Negotiation™ is concerned about, the relationship between you and the other person, and how the outcome will affect the other person. It is based on enhanced people skills or relational skills. Relational skills help people feel good about themselves and their relationship with you. All satisfying relationships are built on respect, appreciation, and concern for the welfare of the other person.

When you have good relational skills, you care about what and how the other person feels. You want them to have pleasant memories about your encounter together. You want them pleased and satisfied so they will buy or interact with you again, you want them to be happy. And Happiness is a feeling people want to share. So they tell their friends and relatives about the good deal (good feeling) they received from you. And if you are in a service business, they will send their friends and relatives to do business with you. Because they want them to experience the same good feeling you gave to them.

Your people skills allow you to establish rapport, trust and friendship with stranger because they like you. But you will need to accept and like yourself before others will accept you. We role model to other people how we feel about ourselves and how we want to be treated. When you like yourself, it is alright to make a mistake and you feel secure within yourself to risk possible rejection or humiliation from others when you reach out to them in a friendship gesture. Because you know your best friend is with you wherever you go; for that friend is you. People are always less fearful when they interact with a trusted friend. And they are more likely to negotiate in good faith.

Soft power negotiating skills is the blending and interplay between your personal skills (belief system about males, females other cultures, your feelings of superiority/inferiority), and your people skills (attitude, self-esteem, fears, level of anxiety).

Whether you are the winner or loser you always profit from every negotiation encounter. You learn what you did that was not in the best interest of all person involved in the negotiation. And you have an opportunity to make corrections the next time you negotiate.

Soft power negotiating skills generate an atmosphere of warmth, caring, and concern that is unobtainable when you use hard power negotiating skills (overpowering, manipulation, deception). Soft power negotiating skills can be learned. If you desire to develop soft power negotiating skills, begin today to become more skilled in the following areas of your personal development:

1. Self-acceptance (self-esteem, belief in self and support of self)

2. Belief system (less restrictive more open to new ideas and belief systems).

3. Attitude (positive vs negative)

4. Authority figures (your feelings towards/about them)

5. Relationship (supportive/antagonistic/isolationist)

6. Power - inner/outer perception how much you possess of each kind of power.

7. Control whether flexible or rigid. If you have a need, or feel a need to control the events of your life, you are likely to be rigid, and if in a negotiation would fight to win as if your life was at stake. And you will feel like a failure if you lost. If you are flexible towards control, you are less likely to view loss of control over circumstances as a personal failure

8. Communication - the way you communicate affects your personal skills and people skills. Your voice tone, timbre, quality, word usage, and diction all determine if you make an emotional connection with others. The more similarity there is between you and the other person, the greater the likelihood of effective and meaningful communication.

9. Self discipline - your ability to manage the negative emotions of fear, resentment, anger, and hate so they do not adversely affect your interactions with others.

10. Your people skills is the ability to use your personality, interactional, interpersonal, and communication skills to connect with others so that the perceived difference between the two of you is minimized. So you are seen as warm, kind cooperative, supportive, and friendly.

What Is Soft Power

Soft power is an inner attitude. It is demonstrated by being focused and totally submerged in the moment, without fear, apprehension, or doubt about the rightness of what one is doing. You are able to deliver your message to others with conviction, compassion and understanding.

Soft Power is a humanistic approach to power. Here you are concerned about the welfare of the person and you seek the best outcome that is fair and just for all. The soft power approach focuses on the development and refinement of your people skills, with emphasis on personal, emotional growth, self discipline and a gentle tone of voice.

It is adding value to the self to deliberately communicate using: softer word selection, lower voice pitch, timbre, intonation, having empathy with others, treating oneself and others with patience, kindness, gentleness and consideration.

Soft Power is Proactive. It changes the way others responds to you. Because you model the behavior you desire to see, through your word choice, voice, pitch, and timbre; to alter your style of personal interaction with others.

Advantages of Soft Power
1. Raises self esteem
2. Creates Bonding these by strengthens, relationships
3. Gives you an option of another way to interact with others
4. Creates a desire to cooperate with others and promotes cooperative behavior

Advantages of Hard Power
1. Quick, expedient, gets job done

SOFT POWER SKILLS, WOMEN AND NEGOTIATIONS

<u>Disadvantage Hard Power</u>
1. Does not create or promote long term relationship or bonding
2. Stifles communication
3. Limit communication and personal interaction

<u>Mental Barriers to Use Soft Power</u>
1. Need to be nice or perceived as nice
2. Need to be accepted/approval
3. Fear of change
4. Fear of becoming too weak or be perceived as weak
5. Low self esteem - fear of risk
6. Lack of self confidence
7. Confused/mixed self image
8. Rigid personality, structured self concept, inability and unwillingness to change, fear losing self

What Is A Soft Power Relationship?

In soft power we are concerned about the relationship between us, the other person and the outcome. Therefore, we take time before we negotiate or speak to establish rapport, trust and friendship. When we feel that we are interacting with a trusted friend, we are likely to be less fearful and more likely to negotiate in good faith.

Soft Power character traits:

Acknowledges one's needs, the needs of others, and seek to meet both. It involves compassionate dealing with oneself and others. We not only care about ourself, but the welfare of others is a concern as well. We are self assured, but we realize that others have rights the same as ours. This person is firm, yet gentle. They do not attempt to control, manipulate or influence others through the use of bribery, manipulation or scare tactics. The person who uses soft power^{TM} stands their ground, peacefully through gentle persuasion or confrontation.

SOFT-POWER

1. Cooperative Endeavor, Goal Is "Win, Win"
2. Respect People, Positive About Them

3. Compassionate, Concerned About Others Feelings
4. Self Assured, With No Fear About Outcome
5. Firm, but Flexible
6. Powerful, No Desire to Control/Manipulate
7. Able to Accept "No" Without Damage to Ego
8. Fair, Seek a Just Outcome

Soft power does not see humility as a character defect or sign of weakness. Humility brings out the best in people because it forces one to practice self discipline and self restraint over one's undesirable urges and impulses. Humility brings forth our inner strength. When we are humble, we are able to recognize our divine nature. When we are in this state of awareness, we can have an experience of being one with God. This feeling of being one with God forces us to behave from this perspective and we are gentler with ourselves and others.

When our thoughts are focused on spiritual matters our thinking shifts to a higher plane of trust and faith in a higher power to guide us. Then our doubts, fears, and suspicions of others are transformed by the renewing of our Christ mind. For as we take on the Christ mind, we relinquish our mortal mind. We no longer have a need for certainty in our life. Because we trust our higher power, we are able to let go our human will to allow God's will to take over. Then we can say "not my will Lord, but let thy will be done in my body, mind and affairs.

We are free from all outer, or personal concerns. And we are able to focus on the divine nature within ourselves and others. When this happens we are filled with awe, wonder and thanksgiving for the divine wisdom that expressing through us, giving us a new vision of people and life.

The development and integration of these character building skills enables you to cope with situations where you feel ridiculed, attacked, intimidated, helpless, hopeless, vulnerable and without support. In soft power, the power resides within you. It is your *inner* emotional strength. You have an inner self discipline and emotional strength that adds value to the communicative process through the use of soft word selection, voice pitch, vocal timbre (medium resonance of vocal overtones), intonation (modulation and inflection of words).

Soft Power is Proactive

Soft power is proactive because you assume responsibility for your actions and you are accountable for the reaction you create. You do not leave things to chance. You think before you speak because you are trying to create the communicative milieu you desire. Your goal is to change the way others respond to you by modeling the behavior you desire them to display. You do this through your word choice, voice pitch, timbre, and alteration in your personal style of interaction.

You deliberately use care to select the word or words you will use to create the emotional state or mood you desire to manifest, through the use of your vocal pitch, timbre, and intonation to create a favorable reaction in the other person.

The use of soft power words allows you to put emphasis on a word or group of words to lessen or to increase the impact of the word to create a given effect or mixed interpretation of a statement. example (close' the door or close! the door!) The latter example gives a forceful inflection to the words and is more likely to evoke anger or suppressed negative feelings and emotions.

Soft Power Words Are:

1. Why don't we…
2. Do you think…
3. You may want to…
4. What would you consider…
5. Maybe…
6. What if
7. We will help you…
8. I'll see what I can do.
9. I'll look into it for you.
10. Please…
11. I understand.
12. Could you…
13. Would you…
14. You might consider…
15. We…
16. Let's…
17. Would you mind…

18. How do you feel?
19. Do you have any thoughts on the matter?
20. What is your opinion?
21. I was wondering…
22. "A penny for your thoughts."

The Key Elements Of Soft Power Are:
1. Clear, open, honest communication
2. Genuine concern and liking of people
3. Seeking a just and fair outcome for all persons involved
4. Humility includes the esteemed qualities of patience, modesty, simplicity, gratitude and quietude.
5. Person has self-discipline; able to control temperament, rage, and control emotions of: frustration, disappointment, anger.

How Does Soft Power Work?

It is the blending and interplay between your personal skills and people skills that allows you to refine your negotiation and communication style. It is the connection you make with people through your use of words, communicative skills, body language, your concern and respect for people and their feelings. This is what people skills are about. In soft power, The focus is on your making a positive and meaningful connection between yourself and other people.

The Factors Involved in Soft Power Negotiation Are:
1. Communication: Listening and acting based on what you hear.
2. Relationship: Open or closed
3. Attitude: Positive or negative
4. Life Position: Powerful or powerless
5. Control or out of control
6. Independent or dependent
7. Choice or no choice.
8. Creativity: Decision to create your life from choice or be a reactionary person.
9. Self Image: Right to have one's needs met; basic rights.
10. Self-Esteem: Self-worth and self-deserving.

11. Self Confidence: Self assurance and the ability to act and behave according to one's belief.
12. Orientation to life: Way you problem solve and resolve conflict, your life pattern.

The Character Traits of Soft Power™ Are:

Soft power is an understanding of the self, to better know how others feel, what they want/desire and how to meet those needs to get what one wants. Soft power can be liken to a tree near the ocean that is firmly rooted, yet pliant enough so that it is neither uprooted nor destroyed by the turbulent winds of a storm. Soft power is a position of inner power and emotional strength grounded in the spiritual truth that you are never alone and that you have the resources within you to confront and conquer any challenge.

In soft power the focus of the *power is inside the person*, whereas in hard power the focus of the *power is outside the person* (power struggle, tug of war, top dog/under dog etc.). Soft power is proactive, because you take responsibility for whatever happens in the negotiation dialogue. You look for ways to make change happen. You do not sit and allow things to happen.

Soft power is a way of interacting with others, and have them feel good about the energy vibrations, and verbal exchange between the two of you. Soft power techniques allow others to perceive you as warm, helpful, and supportive rather than threatening, tricky, or uncooperative. There are several aspects of your personality you can improve, through the incorporation of soft power techniques in your interactions with others so you are experienced more positively.

For rapid results you can attend our weekly: personal development classes, women/men addiction and abuse support groups, women/men domestic violence-anger management support group; our monthly self-esteem, relationship building, or communication skills workshops by calling, Our Place Center of Self-Esteem at (619) 262 9951. Also available are personal phone consultations for 30 and 60 minutes at a modest fee, prepaid or visa/mastercard. If you are unable to do any of the above, here is an over view of things you can do on your own.

Ida Greene, Ph.D.

For best results set aside 20 minutes daily to focus on one of the following areas of personal development, or weekly to improve your skills in the use of soft power^{TM}. They are:

1. Self-Acceptance - Have the ability to be open with others, without feeling guarded, or a need to maintain boundaries between them and others. Feel equal to others, regardless of their differences in ability, attitude, status or position in community/life. Accepts they have a wide range of feelings: love, joy, resentment, anger, rage, sadness, and they are in control of them.

2. Self-Esteem - Have the ability to esteem themselves and others; to look for, express, and expect the best for self and others. They have a firm belief in certain values and principles which they uphold even in the face of strong group opinion. And secure enough to modify their values if new evidence or experience warrants it.

3. Self-Image - the ability to present and project a positive picture of self that is genuine. See themselves as a person of interest and value to others, or their associates.

4. Self-Respect - See themselves as valued, worthwhile and deserving to their needs met. And resist the efforts of others to dominate them. Can accept praise and compliments without feeling guilty or uncomfortable.

5. Self-Confidence – They act on their best judgment, without feeling excessively guilty or regretting their actions even when others disapprove. Do not spend undue time worrying about the past, the present, or the future. Are confident in their ability to deal with problems, failure and setbacks.

6. People Skills - Genuinely enjoy themselves in a variety of activities involving work, play, companionship, idleness, and creative expression. Avoid dominating or controlling the affairs of others. Possess sensitivity to the needs of others, to

their social customs, and have let go the belief, they need to advance at the expense of others.

7. Attitude - You pay close attention that your attitude is one of cooperation and congeniality. Our attitude projects outside us like a ray or aura. Therefore people experience us in a positive or negative manner, and will respond to us in a pleasant or unpleasant way.

USES OF SOFT POWER

Winning Behavior

Soft Power allows you to:
1. Deal successfully with others and feel good about oneself.
2. Involves behaving, doing, saying, acting in a certain way deliberately to shape the behavior of the other person.
3. Tries to change the reality which is causing bad feelings.
4. Deals with reality that the behavior of the person using hard power is aggressive, controlling, intimidating, threatening and may be manipulative.

Winning is Success!

USES OF HARD POWER

Defending Behavior

Hard Power allows you to:
1. Pampers your feelings to lessen hurt caused by others and reality.
2. Involves thinking, feeling, fantasizing, planning, talking to oneself — over and over to convince oneself of the rightness of their actions.
3. Tries to change one's negative feelings towards others by self-justification.
4. Deals with the intellect to avoid feelings. A lack of familiarity or undeveloped skills with feelings generate anxiety.
5. Inability to be gentle or tender with self and/or others.

Defending is Failure

Chapter 6

NON ASSERTION IS NOT SOFT POWER

Non assertion inhibition results in the inability to speak out or act on your own behalf, on behalf of others, on behalf of an idea or value system. Inhibition is based on the premise that your attempts to be assertive will meet with a negative response, and this negative response matters—in other words, you care.

If you predict a negative response but feel it does not matter, you won't be inhibited. But when it does matter to you, the predicted negative response can so influence your behavior that you are prevented from being assertive.

Rational and irrational components to inhibition:

There are a couple of ways to check your reality about facts
1. Ask others how they would behave if placed in this position. If no one else would be inhibited if they were in your place, then you can question the reality of your predictions of a negative response by others to your assertive behavior.

2. Recall the ways yours parents controlled you as a child. Did they show their disapproval by anger, tears, or indifference? Does the anger, tears, or indifference of others still control your behavior now? Visualize the type of negative response you predict your behavior will elicit from others. Do you predict an angry response to your attempts at meeting your needs? Do you now fear most hurting people.

The inhibitory factor in assertion is the displacement of early childhood socialization patterns into the present. Determine which people most inhibit your assertiveness and try to identify what trait in them, reminds you of your parents. It may be a look, a walk, a voice, an expression, or attitude. Are you attributing to a boss, colleague, or subordinate a motive that once belonged to a parent, that now inhibit you.

Ask yourself, if you want to be inhibited by this person who is not your parent? Why not? Write out your answer below.

Now that you have identified this behavioral pattern, chances are that whenever you see this in others it will still influence you. The Only way to deal with non assertion is to keep looking for the pattern so that you can identify it and thus render your unconscious conscious and therefore more under your control.

Advantages of Soft Power Are:
1. Elevate feelings of self-worth and self-importance, thereby raising self-esteem.
2. Creates bonding, which strengthens relationships
3. Gives you options of alternate ways to interact with others
4. Our positive interpersonal interactions, create a desire in others to comply with our requests.
5. Fosters cooperation, because it brings out our best self

Psychological Barriers to Use Soft Power:
1. Negative word associations - We associate the word *soft* with feminine/weakness and *hard* power with masculine/strong.
2. Our need to be accepted/approved.
3. Fear of change.
4. Fear to be weak, or be perceived as weak.
5. Low self-esteem, causes us to be cautious and fear risks.
6. Doubt, lack of trust in one's judgement.
7. Confused/mixed self-image.
8. Rigid personality, structured self concept, inability or unwillingness to change, for fear of losing self.

Power is exhilarating, intoxicating, fearful, frightening, and awesome. Many people want power but they do not want the responsibility it entails. There is a huge responsibility because you often decide the fate or destiny of a persons life or career. Sometimes you are placed in the position of being God like. Then people fear you and like you at the same time. They hate you and love you. They despise you and adore you. And the disappointing aspect of the whole thing is that you will die just as all people. And you may or may not be remembered in a positive way. Some people may be glad when you are dead. And what a sad tribute that would be to your life or your living. As my mother said "what goes around, comes back around to you."

POWER ASSESSMENT
DO YOU HAVE IT?

To assess your power potential, ask yourself these questions
To identify your power sources, answer these questions:

1. Does my superior, co-worker, significant other care about what I think?

2. Has anyone ever asked my opinion about this or another matter?

3. Am I held in high esteem by my superior/s or coworkers?

4. What power or influence do I have? Is there something I can say or do that will make a difference in this outcome?

5. Should I let my thoughts/ideas be known? Why?

6. Is this issue important to me? Have I invested energy and time in the project/task? Do I care about the outcome?

7. What power leverage does the other party have regarding this matter or situation?

8. What can I do to increase my power base (things I need to know to make my decisions).

9. How can I offset any negative aspects of the way the other person uses power.

10. Do I want responsibility (power)?

11. Can I handle all of the tasks/demands this situation may entail?

12. Am I content to be a watcher or do I want to take the risk to be involved/committed?

Affirmations To Heal The Emotions

Today let us concentrate on thoughts of peace and love, knowing there are no greater forces in the world.

If I've had a fall today, I know that picking myself up has strengthened me.

Today I give special attention to that three-letter word F-U-N! Let's have a F-U-N day!

Dolly Sewell, Nottingham, England.

Ida Greene, Ph.D.

Chapter 7

How to Successfully Negotiate Anything

Planning and Preparing for a Negotiation:

1. Knowledge is power. Learn as much as possible about the other person.
2. Consider wants, and needs, yours and the other person.
3. Keep in mind the goals, desired outcome, yours and the other person.

Whenever two people meet to discuss anything, there are six different personalities present. 1. The person "A" actually is. 2. The Person "A" thinks they are. 3. The Person "A" appears to be. The same applies for "B."

Based on what you just learned, how and what would you take into consideration when planning or preparing for a negotiation interaction? Write your answer below -

_____

_____

_____

_____

_____

_____

_____

Ida Greene, Ph.D.

PRINCIPLES OF NEGOTIATION

The goal of all negotiation is to work together with your opposer to solve a problem by mutual effort. It is not a *win/lose* situation. <u>Both you and the other party lose when negotiations become a power play.</u>

Cooperation must be your goal:

1. You must change defensive behavior into supportive communication.

2. If you desire to make changes in your communication, you must also make them in your interpersonal relationships.

3. Always use descriptive language, it gives background information and does not seek to change your opposer.

The secret of negotiation is to find out what you want and ask for it. Then find out what the other person wants and figure out a way to give it to them without depleting yourself.

You have the right to say *no* at any point in a negotiation, whether you explain the reason for the *no* or not. Additionally all agreements are subject to *renegotiation* at any point. <u>What have you learned from this section? Write down your thoughts now.</u>

NEGOTIATION GUIDELINES

1. Try to investigate the issues, rather than take sides on them.

2. Use a problem solving approach rather than to dictate or delegate.

3. Remember that the *relationship* of the parties is always superior to the negotiation. You will never get what you want from another person unless you develop and nurture that relationship. Always keep in mind that you are stranger until

you establish a compatible connection between you and the other person.

4. Sensitivity to the feelings of others and understanding of the situation can have a positive effect on the outcome. <u>Can you think of how you can employ this in your situation?</u>

5. Right timing is a critical factor. Be aware that whenever two people meet, emotions are always in the background. Often the emotions of fear, anxiety, envy, and greed if allowed to surface can create a stumbling block to most well intentioned plans. <u>Have you taken inventory of your emotions? Where do you stand on this matter?</u>

6. Seek to understand and recognize the *needs, desires, and motives* of your opposer.

7. Negotiate in a manner so that your opposer reveals him or herself to you. Ask open ended questions. For example, ask them, what would you like to include in the negotiation/ proposal?

8. Remember to be *cordial, polite and respectful in speech and mannerisms*.

RULES OF NEGOTIATION

1. Establish your objective/s to be negotiated. Keep it in a process state, so that it is open to change. Learn to deal with the objectives of a negotiation as you would with the wind (you never know when it comes or where it goes). This means you may have to shift the focus of your negotiations or deal with an unexpected topic you had not intended. <u>Are you able to do this or are you rigidly locked into maintaining the status quo?</u>

2. Decide if you will be negotiating as an individual or as a team, and also how much authority you can wield individually if a

partnership. It will make a big difference in the speed of the negotiation process if you are unable to make a decision or come to an agreement without the approval of your partner/superior.

3. Ask yourself, what is the issue/s being discussed and what is your position?

    a. If you take a position, *negotiate the problem do not demand it.*

    b. Your bargaining position should conceal as well as reveal your stance. Start out with a general statement that can be narrowed down to the satisfaction of both you and the other party. <u>Write out an opening premise now.</u>

4. Negotiation starts with an assumption about a fact, issue, or position to arrive at a decision or agreement. Assumption-> fact-> issue-> position-> Decision. Take the statement you wrote above and follow this procedure. What position or decision did you achieve based on your generalized opening statement? Write your response

    a. If you desire to change a person's decision, you must first alter their assumption. (reframe or reposition their belief). Help them to see the picture you have in mind. Try this on a friend or associate. Write out now how you plan to do this.

To effectively move through the three stages of negotiation, you need to satisfactorily answer these questions for yourself.

1. What is your personal assessment of the situation?

    Is the situation negotiable?

How much will you need to concede or are you willing to make concessions?

2. What are your bargaining assets?

What tangibles do you have that can be transferred into cash or cash reserves, for the thing/s you would like to have?

3. What are you willing to relinquish or trade?

If you feel that you can not afford to give anything away, your bargaining stance will be seen as weak and ineffective. You must be able to trade off time, money, ideas or anything that can produce money; or you can relinquish some of your materials assets or reposition them to make more money for tangibles you want to have.

4. What are you willing to compromise? How much?

Be willing to give in order to receive. You may need to give first, to show the other person that it is safe. *We never lose*, sometimes it just seems that way. Besides you can always use the practice to better negotiate in the future. <u>Life is about learning; not about arriving at a place of comfort, complacency on being right all the time.</u>

5. Are you aware of the problems and benefits to be *achieved jointly* in your negotiation?

   What can you learn or did you learn from this negotiation experience?

No experience we encounter in life ever leaves us where it found us. Seek to learn from life and people. What else will you do with your life but to impact the life of someone in a positive way, even though they may not view it that way at the time.

THE THREE STAGES OF NEGOTIATION

1. FORMATIVE STAGE - Here the participants are anxious and puzzled. Trust is low and fear high. People may display defensive behavior, and put up barriers to listening.

2. DEVELOPING STAGE - Investigate. Develop and gather your facts. Classify disagreements, look for the cause/s of problem. Rights of the individual emerge here. It is wise to write out issues and points of difference so that all parties can see. We tend to believe what we see in print.

3. UNIFYING STAGE - Seek solutions, compromise, ask the question how can I make the situation, relationship, structure work? Focus on areas of accommodation and cooperation when you negotiate. Look for ways you can speak the same language even though you may be using different words.

THE STEPS OF A NEGOTIATION

1. Discussion and Compromise
   a. Describe the situation/s you find agreeable/disagreeable.
   b. Explain your feelings using "I" statements.

c. Accept/acknowledge the consequences of your decisions and accept responsibility for your behavior/decision.

2. Fact Find—Determine the facts. What are the issues your concerns?
   A. Meeting preparation and opening
      a. Try to dissolve and dispose of minor issues first, then major ones. *Move in stages and degrees toward an agreement.*

      b. All assumptions have roots in emotional conflict, dogma, and misinformation. *Our beliefs are based on assumptions*, assumed knowledge, not facts.

      c. Be aware of your assumptions as well as those of the other party.

      d. Flaws and blocks occur when you act and think as if an assumption is *true*.

      e. Hidden assumptions - verify the assumptions of both you and the other party. Ask yourself if there is a discrepancy? If so, how wide is the variation?

3. Problem Solve—Set forth as many creative solutions to the problem as possible. Discuss them and, be open to change your position if necessary.

4. State your Position—Neither side should present the best or only solution. Be clear and concise in what you say. If there is confusion here, it will be difficult to clear it up later in the negotiations.

   A. Bidding -
      a. Begin bidding high to allow for adjustments in bartering. In some negotiations there is nothing to bid on/for because that was not set forth in your initial opening statement.

b. Don't threaten or intimidate. This creates a hostile environment that could backfire on you later when you may want the other party to cooperate.

c. Avoid a "take-it-or-leave it position". Most people don't like to be intimidated and will do anything to save face, even if it means prolonged fruitless debating and arguments.

5. Solution—<u>Look for similarities</u>, rather than differences. This helps you to focus on cooperative behaviors as opposed to antagonist conflict and behaviors. *Be a good listener.* <u>Think about ways you could be a better listener. Write down your comments.</u>

   A. Agreeing - How to get agreement:
      a. State your desire

      b. State what you heard the other person say. Ask for confirmation.

      c. Restate again, asking for clarity and agreement.

      d. Set the stage for *future contact* (If needed). Make a statement about a possible meeting if something needs to be clarified or is not satisfactory to an associate/partner who was unable to attend a meeting.

6. Creativity—Try to involve everyone in the process of creative solutions. Allow each person time to offer suggestions. Come up with as many alternatives as possible. It is better to have too many options and to scale down rather than to have a few options that you fight over. When we involve people to find a solution to a problem it allows them to feel that they are making a contribution, and is valuable to the process. <u>Take some time now to make notations on your progress thus far.</u>

How to Successfully Negotiate Anything

The negotiation process is a continuous learning experience. It requires you to understand your actions and reactions, to better understand the behavior of others. There is a relationship between getting our needs met and negotiation. Create an outline to guide you, start with the basic facts that underlie all negotiation, and the principles of negotiation. Next include the Negotiation guidelines to serve as map to point you in the right direction. Then identify the medium of exchange and other factors that can affect the outcome of the negotiation such as non-verbal communication and non-verbal expression. Next list the rules of negotiation, and the three stages of negotiation. Your negotiation plan should include the following:

1. <u>**The Steps of a Negotiation**</u>
   A. **Discussion and Compromise**
   B. **Fact Finding- What are the issues of concern?**
   C. **Problem Solve**--Set forth as many creative solutions to the problem as possible. Discuss them and, be open to change.
   D. **State your Position**--Neither side should present the best or only solution. Be clear and concise in what you say.
   E. **Solutions--<u>Look for similarities</u>, rather than differences.** This helps you to focus on cooperative behaviors as opposed to antagonist conflict and behaviors. *Be a good listener*.
   F. **How to Get Agreement:**
   a. State your desire
   b. State what you heard the other person say. Ask for confirmation.
   c. Restate again, asking for clarity and agreement.

Ida Greene, Ph.D.

Chapter 8

THE FIVE NEGOTIATION STYLES

Our style of negotiation is like a trademark. It allows others to gauge or predict how we will likely act or react if we are presented with similar circumstances. The first land mark is related to our self-esteem, and then to our behavior. Our self-esteem is so much a part of our emotional fabric that it is hard to peel away from the core of our being. When you operate from a win/lose premise, you see things in polarities of black or white concepts. There are no shades of gray or allowance for mistakes or errors. In fact ambiguity is not tolerated. These persons are very guarded and protective. May act defensive when confronted, due to a low sense of self-esteem. The categories on the left is indicative of your behavior and the categories on the left show your degree of self-esteem or self-value.

1. Win/Lose   Low self-esteem

2. Accommodate   Empowers

3. Withdraws   Low self-esteem

4. Compromise (Victim)   low-self esteem

5. Collaborate   Empowers

The negotiation styles correspond to how you may behave or react when confronted with a challenge or when under attack.

The Five Negotiation Styles

Pushy Style - Aggressive behavior, "I take, I want it my way attitude." Win/Lose

Hold Back Style - "Prove it to me, come to me, I am standing my ground, don't budge position." Withdraw

Buddy Style - "Let's be pals. Let us share what you have philosophy." Accommodate

Check-It-Out Style - "I will check it out first, I will test things to see how far I can go, bluff, game player." Compromise

Non Resistive Style - "I hold myself and you blameless." Let's work together to solve the problem Collaborate or get a Resolution

NEGOTIATION STRATEGIES AND TACTICS

<u>Strategies And Tactics You Can Employ In Your Negotiations</u>:

1. Develop power and influence through the people you know.

2. Use the emotions of love and concern to persuade.

3. Test assumptions that block progress for clarity. Ask questions to see if there is be a misinterpretation.

4. Use the power of suggestion to state your position in the most favorable way.

5. Positioning, state your position in a clear, concise manner. Watch grammar, diction, and tone of voice.

6. Compromise early in the negotiations to show your willingness to bargain in good faith. This leaves the door open to cooperative behavior and positions you in a favorable light. However, if the other party takes this as a sign of weakness, you can always point to the fact that you are willing to cooperate and you made the first move in that direction. If the opposition continues to be stubborn and refuses to budge continue to remind them that you want to cooperate and you took corrective towards that end.

Deception is not a tactic and should never be used. Stop and write out a problem real or perceived. Then select one of the above strategies to handle the problem. What will you say?

BEHAVIOR OF DIFFERENCES

WINNING BEHAVIOR

1. Deals successfully with others and feels good about oneself.

2. Involves behaving, doing saying, acting

3. Tries to change the reality which is causing the bad feelings

4. Deals with reality

5. Enjoys life

DEFENDING BEHAVIOR

1. Pampers ones feelings to lessen hurt caused by others and reality

2. Involves thinking, feeling, fantasy, planning, talking to oneself, over and over!

3. Tries to change feelings by doing something "nice" for oneself"

4. Deals with feelings

5. Suffers and complains constantly to others

PATIENCE

The qualities of patience and understanding are much needed in our world. I contribute to the fulfilling of this need by being patient with myself, others, and I give understanding to all.

My capacity for patience increases as I express an attitude of understanding.

I find new understanding and greater insight in my daily giving and living by having a patient attitude.

Patience and understanding contribute to the sharing of my thoughts and ideas with others. And the relationships in my life are blessed because of this.

Being patient and understanding, gives me a greater sense of oneness with God.

I realize it is the Universal mind of God that is working in and through me to establish love, harmony, and understanding.

In my steadfast and appreciative approach to life. I make a valuable contribution to my world, and all people every where.

Chapter 9

Manage Conflict And Anger To Move Through Negotiation

Our Cultural communication and attitudes condones the use of confrontation to solve conflict caused by our differences and disputes. Conflict is the breakdown in communication between two or more people, and is often expressed as disagreement, power struggle, or a fight. Our feelings are an index to our inner needs and frustrations. When we have intense feelings like anger, resentment, and rage we tend to act them out.

Our society has learned to handle conflict and disagreements through anger, verbal conflict and physical violence. Some of cliches' that support violence are: "only the strong survive, make my day, keep a stiff upper lip, big boys don't cry,"

Dr. Albert Ellis feels we have to change our belief system to change our expression of anger. He talks about the ABC'S of Anger.

- A - The activating event, something that happens to trigger our anger.
- B - The belief system you have about the activating event. Do you believe this activating event is a good thing.
- C - The consequence of the belief of our emotional response. ex. sadness, disappointment, or happiness.

Anger is one of the emotions we express that continues to get us in trouble with others. It is an emotion with great energy. Anger can cause emotional damage to us, and others if it is uncontrolled or misdirected. We need to learn to channel our anger energy into a constructive outlet.

We can not avoid conflict in life, and because we differ, we rarely see things the same. There will always be things people do, or say that will frustrate or irritate us. It is our expectation of people, situations, and ourselves that acts as a stimulus to cause us to respond angrily to a situation. There is always a split second following an event that makes us angry, when we can be aware of our anger and redirect it. If you are not in charge of your anger, it will control and consume you. Therefore you must learn to be in control of yourself to manage your anger. You are responsible for your life situations, and the response you make to them. Ask yourself, what is the gap between what you expect and what you are receiving?

Anger is a valuable signal, because it lets us know when something is wrong and needs to be corrected. The critical factor is whether your expression of anger is adding to the problem or helping to solve it. **Often when we are angry, one or more of these things are going on**:

1. We want something and are not getting it.
2. From past experience, we expect trouble.
3. We feel powerless to get what we want.

The premise of anger management techniques is for you to use your anger as a signal to identify your problem and deal with it. Rather than act upon your anger by lashing out, to make the situation worse, or to hold your angry feelings inside.

Anger can lead to: 1. Angrily Lash out—> To make the situation worse
2. Hold feelings inside—> Creates resentment, physical symptoms

Or

3. You can identify the problem to handle. You do this by changing the way you think, your beliefs. This is helpful when t hinking about something that irritates you or makes you mad. Because whenever you fight fire with fire, someone will get burned.

When a situation provokes you and you are preparing to respond, begin thinking and ask yourself some critical questions.

1. How can I manage this situation?
2. What is it that I absolutely have to do?
3. Have you decided how you will regulate your anger?
4. Will an argument between you and the other person solve your problem?
5. Do you have a way to get time to calm down or relax?

Alternatives To Angrily Acting Out
1. Take time to **rethink** about what provokes you.
2. Use a planned relaxation technique
3. Stay calm and keep your cool
4. Ask yourself if you are overreacting, taking thing too seriously, or justifying your right to be angry.

Basic Concepts To Understand to Manage Anger

1. Anger is an emotion
2. Reason is not employed when we are angry.
3. Anger is the results of jumping to conclusions about an outcome.
4. Anger creates a sense of energy, excitement and negative aliveness
5. Anger is self serving
6. Anger is addictive
7. Anger is about power and control
8. Anger is used to intimidate, instill fear, and as an outlet to get rid of one's inner poison/toxins.
9. You do not have a license to hurt or abuse another with your anger.
10. No one has given you permission to hurt them because of your inability to handle you life's problems.
11. When you are angry, you are out of control, not the other person.

12. Others may provoke you to anger, but you do not have to respond angrily. When you do what others want they have the power to control you.
13. No one is the cause of you responding angrily. You have freedom of choice.
14. When you get mad, you are exercising power or seeking to avenge yourself.
14. You get some pleasure from hurting others, if you get angry repeatedly.
15. If you get angry repeatedly, you are unable to control your feelings of anger.
16. Are you in control of your anger or does it control you? If you drew a picture of your anger, how would it look. Draw a picture of your anger below.

Chapter 10

Use Soft Power To Resolve Conflict
SOFT POWER NEGOTIATION SKILLS

What Is It?

It is an understanding of the self to know how others feel, what they want, and desire. You look at ways to meet their needs to get what you want. It's the use of soft words that supports and enhances the total person. Soft power is relationship oriented. You avoid the use of words that are caustic, inflammatory that provokes incites, or invoke another person to respond angrily to what you say.

How Does It Work?

Everything we do is negotiation. All human relationships revolve around barter and exchange. Therefore all interpersonal interactions entail negotiation. It is the blending and interplay between your *personal skills and people skills* that allows you to get what you want from others and have them feel good about the communication exchange.

HARD POWER NEGOTIATION

1. Tough - no compassion
2. Dominant - controls, rule
3. Forceful - coercion, fear
4. Aggressive - verbal/physical abuse
5. Attacking - confront, critical, condemns
6. Intimidates - frightens, bully
7. Takes what is not it's own

SOFT POWER NEGOTIATION

1. Acknowledges It's needs/ others'
2. Compassionate with self and others.
3. Caring
4. Self assured, deserving, self worth

5. Firm, yet gentle.
6. Does not seek to control, manipulate or bribe.
7. Stands its ground, peacefully
8. Seeks a just outcome.
9. Is powerful lovingly

Conflict Resolution

Conflict is the result of ineffective communication between individuals. This breakdown in communication is often expressed as disagreement, friction, or power struggle. Effective communication can ease tensions in relationships to provide rules and guidelines to follow that provides clarity and understanding. When we are truthful with ourself and others about our purpose and intent for our communication, others can relax because they know we have their best interest in mind.

Types of Conflict

There are many types of conflict. They are special interest, values, personal friction, and interpersonal conflict.

Special Interest - A who gets what situation. One group favors one thing while another wants something different.

Values - Conflict here is based on different values which may be based on professional conduct or a code of ethics.

Personal Conflict - A. Poor communication can be a factor. Other factors are: B. Misinterpretations or stereotypes, which prevent people from seeing another person's point of view. C. Inability to respect the views/rights of others. D. Domineering attitudes or behaviors. E. Expression of negative emotions like anger and resentment.

Interpersonal Conflict - A. Being opinionated or bull headed.
B. Strong willed individuals who are into power and control.
C. Persons who have a "need" to be right all the time.

Note three conflicts you have encountered and offer three solutions to those conflicts.

Conflicts	Solutions
1.	1.
2.	2.
3.	3.

The underlying cause of conflict between most individuals is the use of illogical thinking or irrational thought patterns in their communications. If event A (frown on face) occurs, it does not necessarily mean that B (disapproval) will follow.

When there is conflict between two people, one or more of the following are present: communication breakdown, anxiety, fear, perception by one or both parties that there is in harmony, verbal or nonverbal disagreement, suppressed or overt anger.

Some of the physiological symptoms you may notice may be: A tightness of the muscles in the throat, neck or shoulders; tightness of the jaw bone; rapid breathing or heart beat; gastrointestinal distress; such as belching, acidic stomach, abdominal craps, or diarrhea.

What are some of the behaviors you experience that indicates to you that there is conflict between you and another person?

How does your body react when you are in conflict with another person? List your bodily reactions below:

Example: I am aware that I tighten my shoulders during a verbal altercation with another person.

1.

2.

3.

4.

5.

Some of the things I can/will do to lessen or prevent conflict with others are:

Coping mechanism I can employ to manage stress or prevent conflict is: Example - become aware of my illogical or irrational thought patterns.

My Plan Of Action To Handle Conflict

In conflicts, I shall refrain from being aggressive.

Example - I will avoid:

1. Raising my voice
2. Being demanding
3. Attacking

List things that you will do to refrain from being aggressive.

I will avoid:

1.

2.

3.

4.

5.

6.

7.

Communication is a simple yet complex process. Often the message we send to an individual is received differently than intended and may have a connotation other than the one you sent. Learn how to use "soft power" in your communication, to send a clear, powerful message that has warmth, clarity and impact.

Clear communication decreases conflict and promotes harmonious relations between people. Use active listening, to incorporate "soft power" into your verbal dialogue.

Communication that is misinterpreted can be a source of organizational confusion, tension and conflict. Learn how to send clear, powerful messages with impact that delivers the message you intended. These are the tools you need to express your ideas in a clear, crisp, manner so others hear and understand you:

1. Assessment and knowledge of your communication style
2. Problem solving strategies
3. Decision making that is free of conflict or stress
4. Ability to use your style of communication with self-confidence and impact. Use your listening and people skills to create win-win situations.

Conflict is the breakdown in communication between two or more people, and is often expressed as disagreement, power struggle, or fight. Effective communication can ease tensions and set people on a path of openness, clarity and truthfulness when interacting with each other in the work setting. Remember to differentiate between your intent and effect you desire to see.

To resolve conflicts, you will need to be aware of one's cultural ground, non-verbal communication (body language), non-verbal expressions or a strong desire for personal power.

Communicating to get your message across is essential to your success in all aspects of your daily life. Each of us use words to express our thoughts and feelings through one or more representational system. The three channels through which we process information are, visual, auditory and kinesthetic. Do you know which system you use? Do you speak one way and behave another way?

The way we communicate, words we use, gestures we employ, tone of voice, mannerism and idiosyncrasies all make a statement about who you are. And sends a non-verbal message to others about us. This can be to our advantage or to our disadvantage. Naturally, you prefer it to be to your advantage.

Learn how to communicate so that others get the message you intended to send rather a confused message, a double message, or no message. State your messages in a clear, succinct manner, with feeling so people react positively upon what you say, rather than react in a negative manner to what you say.

Effective communication is the use of select words in an organized, deliberate order, designed to elicit a positive response or behavior from an individual so they get your message and positively respond.

We communicate in three ways. The three forms of communication are 1. Monologue –One-way communication, inner message to the self 2. Dialogue-Two-way communication, outer communication, message between two people. 3. Interpersonal Dialogue- Communication between three or more persons.

The three types of communication are: 1. Verbal 2. Non-verbal 3. Creative. The communication process of transmission channels to communication imparts a message through the written, and spoken language. This can be expressive language in the form of drama, music, and language.

The basic communication process uses spoken language in the following manner:
Sender—> Message—> Receiver—> Decode—> Feedback

The strategies to employ to facilitate communication are problem solving and decision-making. Give feedback that supports others, that is honest, with language that builds and support. Remember to think before you speak. Your, timing and intention, is critical. Your ability to know when to omit or leave something not said shows your grace, style, and refinement as a person.

To get the best from others, communicate to show caring, empathy and concern. Continually seek to get the best from yourself.

And realize that your potential is unlimited, and your finest hour is yet to come.

We have many feelings that can hamper our effectiveness in the negotiation process. Below are feelings people have but fail to recognize or identify. Circle the ones you feel now; and write "N" next to the circle word. If you have felt this way in the past, write past or "P" next to the circled word.

FEELINGS

Abandoned	Cheerful	Envious
Adequate	Childish	Evil
Adamant	Combative	Excited
Affectionate	Competitive	Exhausted
Agony	Condemned	Fascinated
Ambivalent	Confused	Fearful
Angry	Contented	Foolish
Annoyed	Cruel	Frantic
Anxious	Crushed	Frustrated
Apathetic	Deceitful	Frightened
Awed	Defeated	Free
Bad	Delighted	Fury
Beautiful	Desirous	Glad
Betrayed	Despair	Good
Bitter	Destructive	Gratified
Bold	Determined	Guilty
Bored	Different	Gullible
Brave	Diminished	Happy
Burdened	Discontented	Hate
Calm	Distracted	Helpful
Capable	Disturbed	Helpless
Captivated	Dominated	High
Challenged	Divided	Homesick
Charmed	Eager	Honored
Charming	Ecstatic	Horrible
Cheated	Empty	Hurt
Challenged	Energetic	Hysterical

Ignored	Nervous	Satisfied
Ignorant	Nice	Scared
Imposed	Nutty	Screwed up
Impressed	Obnoxious	Sexy
Infatuated	Obsessed	Shocked
Infuriated	Odd	Silly
Inspired	Outraged	Sneaky
Intimidated	Overwhelmed	Spiteful
Isolated	Pain	Stingy
Jealousy	Panicky	Stupid
Joyous	Peaceful	Tempted
Jumpy	Persecuted	Tense
Kind	Pity	Terrible
Keen	Pleased	Terrified
Lazy	Pressured	Tired
Lecherous	Pretty	Trapped
Left out	Proud	Troubled
Lonely	Quarrelsome	Ugly
Love	Queer	Violent
Loving	Rage	Vehement
Low	Rejected	Wicked
Lustful	Relaxed	Wonderful
Mad	Relieved	Weepy
Mean	Remorse	Worry (ied)
Miserable	Restless	Yucky
Mystical	Righteous	Zapped
Naughty	Sad	Zingy

POSITIVE ASSERTION

Use Positive Assertion To Go After What You Want

The characteristic of positive assertion is powerful communication, authenticity (being genuine in our feelings), and empowerment (activities designed to increase one's personal position of power). Often our failure to assert ourselves is a fear of the unknown, or a perceived failure due to faulty reasoning. When we fear the worst, we create an expectant state of mind that helps to bring about the situation. If we fear a person or situation, we are repelled to move towards the person or situation. This lessens our personal power base and impedes our drive to go forward to complete a given task. To employ positive assertion, we have to take action in spite of our fears or imagined fears of failure or ruin.

Advantages of Soft Power

Soft power negotiation skills, is based on enhanced people skills. To use soft power skills you want to develop the ability to relate with people, so they are willing to share valuable information with you. If people feel comfortable when with you, they are more likely to tell you personal information. Try to be friendly, become a friend, and strive to be perceived as a friendly person.

How to be positively assertive in your job to get what you want:
1. Set realistic goals
2. Maintain a positive attitude
3. Take positive steps to cope with your fears.
4. Use positive assertion to increase your positive power base.
5. Organize your day into the following categories of tasks on
   <u>A. Things To Do Today Pad, label them</u>:
   A. Personal b. Professional c. Social d. Spiritual.

Check them off as they are completed (+1) for each activity under each category you do. And place a "0" beside it (i.e., Social 0), If you will not be doing an activity under that category for the day. For example:

THINGS TO DO TODAY

Personal - Get clothes from the Cleaner +1
Professional - Type Resume (did not get accomplished) 0
Social - watched T.V. for 3 hours. (+3)
Spiritual - Read affirmations, read Bible, take a walk to get in touch with my higher power. +2 (did not read Bible)

At the end of each day, tally the number of personal +1, professional 0, social +3, or spiritual activities +2. This way you can see where you devoted most of your time each day.

Use this page to help you look at ways you can positively assert yourself to get your needs met. This may mean that you may have to negotiate or trade off something at work or at home. Do the exercise below. Prioritize activities from 1 to 8.

<u>Write down a typical day for yourself. How could you use positive assertion to negotiate for more time to complete a task that is high on your priority list of "things to do today list?</u>

1. _____

2. _____

3. _____

4. _____

5. _____

6. _____

7. _____

8. _____

Affirmations To Heal The Emotions

I express my gratitude to "anon," the author of so many worthwhile verses and songs: "Coming together is a beginning. Keeping together is progress. Working together is success.

I greet this new month with joy. I think of each new day as a jewel to be polished.
Today I adopt Admiral Perry's slogan: "I'll find a way or make one." He was the first to discover the North Pole.

Dolly Sewell, Nottingham, England.

Ida Greene, Ph.D.

Chapter 11

IDENTIFY YOUR NEGOTIATION STYLE TO RECOGNIZE
AND RESPOND TO THE STYLE OF OTHERS

Our negotiation style is the behavior we display and use when we problem solve. There is never a right way or best way to arrive at an agreement. The beliefs we hold about people who are unlike us in behavior, appearance or attitude can impede our ability to negotiate if we carry our culture with us as baggage. Our culture is like luggage and we must carry it lightly wherever we go. Every situation is different and you may need to employ a different tactic in every case. *We are creatures of habit.* Therefore, it is easy for us to become enmeshed in routine automatic behaviors and think that there is only one way to solve a problem.

There are as many ways to solve a problem, as there are people. We need to keep an *open mind* and seek to share as well as learn from others. Allow other people a chance to help you solve your problems; *two heads are always better than one in many cases.* The goal is to problem solve. The two keys to problem solving that will improve your negotiation skills are <u>collaboration and compromise</u>.

1. Think of ways you could collaborate or compromise with someone right now to get what you want or position yourself so the likelihood is increased favorably to your advantage.

2. What is your style of negotiation? Write down the answers to both of these now.

Ida Greene, Ph.D.

TO BETTER UNDERSTAND YOUR NEGOTIATION STYLE, ANSWER THE QUESTIONS LISTED BELOW

SELF-DESCRIPTION

Who am I? I am a

What/who am I like?

How do others perceive me?

What are my strengths as a person?

What are my weaknesses?

In what areas do I want to develop greater skills? Now, sit down and summarize what you have learned about yourself. In the following space, write a description of what you are like. Use the five questions stated above as a guide.

Would you want to negotiate with the person you just wrote about?

Why?

State the pros vs. cons.

Mental Treatment For Right Relationships

I want to bless the people I deal with. I want to feel good about all my relationships. I now speak my word for complete peace of mind and ease in all my relationships. The God in me is one with the God in all my relationships. And the God in me is one with the God in all people. I believe this wholeheartedly and I accept this. I relate in a healthy manner to everyone I encounter today. If this includes someone who usually irritates me, I will refuse to let this happen. I will be in control of my emotions, rather than let the other person control my emotions. I affirm right now, that GODs' love through me is already blessing the person/s I have in mind.

Ida Greene, Ph.D.

ASSESS YOUR POTENTIAL FOR POWER NEGOTIATION

This 20 verb list describes some of the ways people feel and act from time to time. Think of your behavior in interaction with other people. How do you feel and act with other people?

Check the five verbs which best describe your behavior in interaction with others as you see it. Then rank these in priority 1 - 5, with "1" being more like me.

acquiesces	disapproves
advises	evades
agrees	initiates
analyzes	judges
assists	leads
concedes	obliges
cooperates	relinquish
coordinate	resists
criticizes	retreats
directs	withdraws

SOFT POWER SKILLS, WOMEN AND NEGOTIATIONS

To Assess Your Power Potential In Negotiations, Ask Yourself These Questions. Write Your Answers Below.

1. What power do I have?

2. What power does the other party have? What power do I have? How can I use this to my advantage?

3. What can I do to increase my power base (things I need to know/do to make my decisions)?

4. How can I offset any negative aspects of the way the other person uses power? Be specific, what can you do?

To determine how you use power, ask yourself these questions. You may write in the book. Think of a situation where you can employ the principles just discussed in the above paragraph.

1. What power do I have?

   a. What aspect of my presentation needs improvement?

2. What power does the other party have? Think of a situation you are currently confronting or have encountered previously.

   a. Ask yourself what power do I have? Write it down.

3. What can I do to increase my power base? What things do I need to know or do before I make my decision?

4. How can I offset any negative aspects of the way the other person uses power.

The amount and kind of power we have is always relative and situational to meet the need and demands in our life at the moment. Therefore the amount of power available to us at any given moment is relative and may be wrongly perceived by us as adequate or inadequate. When we are in the throes of a behavioral activity, our critical assessment skills may be inaccurate. Often our fear level increases, which further impedes our ability to accurately gauge our power potential. Since our cultural orientation to the use of power is hard power; we may find ourselves using hard power, when we think we are using soft power.

We teach and perpetuate violence through our words, voices, and actions. We have culturally learned patterns for how to get what we want. These learned patterns may be maladaptive and ineffective. Besides power, other factors that determine our capacity to negotiate are: self-esteem, self-confidence, manipulation, level of anxiety, people skills, amount of perceived power, and degree of risk taking behavior.

Let's look at the interrelationship between these character traits and the development of soft power negotiating skills.

Self-Esteem—Our self-image is the beliefs/attitudes we hold about ourselves and the ways we think others see us. Most of us have a mental picture of what we feel that we can/will are capable of accomplishing. Often our behavior is overshadowed by a distorted self-perception that allows us to act timid or mediocre. Our self-esteem is important and we must work continuously to maintain a healthy self-image.

There will always be negative factors in our lives which if not controlled will erode the positive beliefs we hold about ourselves. If you are treated with disdain and disrespect often, you may come to believe there is something intrinsically wrong with you. People who feel they are unworthy or undeserving are less likely to negotiate on their behalf. Or if they do, they may be willing to accept far less than they should.

Self-Confidence—The way we behave and what we feel ourselves capable of doing based on the beliefs we/others hold about us. Our self-confidence allows us to move forward with boldness of character acting on a belief that we can accomplish what we set out to do. We can allow it to be o.k. for us to make a mistake, and not have all the answers.

Manipulation—Women are taught as girls to please others for the satisfaction of their needs. This forces them to look outside themselves for the satisfaction of their needs. Also societal/cultural upbringing, and adult role models teach girls to use subtlety, and sexual innuendos to fulfill their wishes and desires. This prevents them from utilizing objective data in their immediate environment, so they resort to prior dysfunctional child like behavior patterns.

Anxiety Level—Our anxiety level may be the result of several factors: low self-esteem, lack of self-confidence, inadequate people skills and poor coping skills due to a dependence on manipulative behaviors. Action cures anxiety and fear. When we take positive action our anxiety decreases and our fears subside.

People Skills—Your people skills is your ability to interact with others on a basis of genuine concern and care for both your welfare and theirs. Practice daily to improve your communication and people skills. Your success as a negotiator is dependent on a proper blending of self-esteem, self-confidence, managing your level of anxiety, your amount of perceived power, your degree of risk taking behavior, and your ability to negotiate rather than manipulate. **It is more powerful to reach a resolution of the problem, rather than a compromise**. Write down now the area/s you need to improve to feel/be more powerful in your negotiation with others.

HOW TO ENHANCE YOUR NEGOTIATING STYLE

Our negotiation style is a composite behavioral characterization of the roles we play in life and a reflection of the many faces we wear. We move in and out of roles through out the day, depending upon the people and circumstances we encounter. This requires flexibility and a willingness to learn about ourselves and others to become a skilled negotiator. It may require that we create a new role, or modify our present way of interacting so that we are able to adapt to a new person or situation. Whether we realize it or not, we are forever creating. Most of us resort to prior learned behavioral patterns. We do not change our behavior unless highly motivated to do so. To change, there has to be a payoff that is to our advantage or perceived by us to be in our best interest.

To understand our style of negotiation, we must be aware of our intentions, values, and our non-verbal communication. Our non verbal communication, often referred to as body language reveals a lot of information about us to another person. Are you aware of your body language? What messages are you sending to others? We send messages to others through our gestures - eye movement, frown on face, tight jaws, pursed lips etc. Through our body movement, we communicate to others, that we are afraid, threatened, hostile, aggressive or friendly.

How well do you know yourself? What unspoken message/s are you sending to others? Are others getting the message you want them to get? Take a moment now and reflect on your body language. Write down how you perceive yourself, then ask an acquaintance to give you feedback about your body language.

WAYS TO ENHANCE YOUR NEGOTIATING STYLE

1. Communicate - Assertively speak with authority, confidence, and without belittling the other person.

2. Be Authentic - Be authentic, real, tell the truth to yourself and others, let what you say be valid.

3. Be Congruent - Behave the same all the time. Do not be inconsistent.

4. Keep a diary of your negotiation activity and change when appropriate.

5. Practice listening, editing what you are going to say and do before you respond.

6. Seek a mentor or coach and practice your negotiation skills with them.

7. Sit down now and write out what you will do to enhance your style of negotiating.

Problem Solving Guidelines

1. Clarify the Interest.

2. Identify the Options.

3. Formulate alternatives to evaluate deal cooperatively.

4. Select a best priority from both your and the other person's perspective.

We Want	They Want

The Possibilities
Major Options

Ida Greene, Ph.D.

Chapter 12

BLOCKS TO DEVELOPING SOFT POWER SKILLS

There are many factors that may impede your ability to develop, or use soft power negotiation skills in your personal life and business affairs. On a scale of 1-10 you will need to score a 10 in the following areas. And the only person who can provide your score is you. This means you will need to develop a high degree of objectivity and introspection to detect your deficiencies. **These are some areas you will need to improve before you can score one hundred in your negotiations**:

1. Personal Development a. Poor self-image b. Self-Rejection c. Others negative reflections of you d. Defensiveness

2. Beliefs you embrace about: a. Your degree of closeness to people. b. Your belief about power and money. c. Set belief that males are: strong, knowledgeable, to be respected, have power d. Females are weak, emotional, not to be trusted, powerless.

3. Is your attitude based on: a. Conflict b. Struggle c. Do you see others as a foe or the enemy.

4. Your image of authority figures; your feelings about them.

5. Fear - Your level of trust in people.

6. Your Relationships, do they tend to be: a. Antagonistic b. Based on a push/pull effect c. Rebellious d. Defiant

7. Is your concept of power a struggle, or tug of war affair.

Ways to Develop Soft Power

In a win negotiation you want the person to walk away feeling they have gained or won something. You will need to get "no's" in negotiation, so learn now to become comfortable hearing "no." We negotiate or barter and trade with people every day.

If you are married or in a relationship, you often need to discuss and trade off what you want for what the other person wants to do or have. If you have children, or you are acquainted with children you can learn a lot about negotiation. Children are good at negotiation. They often use guilt to obtain their desired goal.

Soft power negotiation skill engages every aspect of your being at any given moment. You have to put your personal agenda on hold, when you are looking for the best outcome for both yourself and the other person. You are looking for a solution that honors both you and the other person. The following are areas of your personality, or thing you can do to develop your soft power skills:

1. a. Self-Acceptance b. Learn to be open and have boundaries with others. This requires you know when to say yes, and when to say no. Both are useful and necessary for balance.
2. Harmonize your relationships and be supportive of others.

3. Relinquish Control, give up the need to be right, or get your way all the time. Let go the issues of power and control. Be willing to lose to win.

4. Communication - What you say is as just important as how it is said. Therefore pay close attention to the following aspects of your speaking and speech pattern - a. Voice quality, tone, pitch, word usage b. Clarify "you" statements

5. Power - Change your view of power from struggle to cooperation a. Gently persuade, easy does it.

6. People Skills - Your interpersonal skills with others. Are you seen as a friend or a warring partner when interacting with others.

7. Self Discipline - Involves a good mixture of being in control of bothersome emotions like anger, resentment, hate, envy and jealousy.

8. Attitude - Your attitude is a reflection of your inner state of mind. A healthy attitude is one that says: a. I'm O.K, and so are you. b. Mutual benefit c. Does not have to be win/lose, either/or

The Relationship Between
Getting Our Needs Met And Negotiation

We must understand both our needs and the needs of others to be effective as a negotiator. You must know your needs before you can attend to the needs of others. Do the exercises below to determine your needs:

1. What do you desire to have or would like to get?

2. Do you know what are the needs of the other person you will be negotiating with or confronting? What do they want from you?

3. Identify the Medium of Exchange in a Negotiation (desire, need unmet etc.) No one will ever want the exact same thing as you.

Hidden Agendas in Negotiation

Unconscious (unaware) Drives can be a Motivator of Behavior. Some of the common ones are:

1. Repression (convenient forgetting of an unpleasant past event or future event).

2. Displacement (taking out our anger and aggression on persons or objects that is not the cause of our difficulty).

3. Rationalization-to interpret things in a manner that justifies your behavior.

4. Projection-To attribute your motives to others. Example, to accuse someone of being money hungry, when it is really us.

Conscious (aware) Drives Present in Negotiations Are:

1. Revenge, wounded pride etc.

2. Jealousy (wanting to do what another is doing or wanting what another has)

3. Greed-wanting to outdo others, be on top.

Analyze Your Speech Pattern For Signs Of Antagonism

Very Often I Hear Myself Saying:

1.

2.

3.

A Plan of Action to Increase the Use of Soft Power Techniques

In the future to solve this problem I shall:

1.

2.

3.

Beginning Date:

A PLAN OF ACTION TO HANDLE CONFLICT

The underlying cause of conflict between most individuals is the use of illogical thinking or irrational thought patterns in their communications. If event A (frown on face) occurs, it does not necessarily mean that B (disapproval) will follow.

When there is conflict between two people, one or more of the following are present: communication breakdown, anxiety, perceived fear, by one or both parties that there is disharmony, verbal or nonverbal disagreement, suppressed or overt anger.

In conflicts, I will endeavor to be assertive and refrain from aggressive behavior. To do this I will avoid:

1. Raising my voice
2. Being demanding
3. Attacking what the other person says or their character.

List things you will do to refrain from being aggressive in your transactions with others. I will avoid:

1.

2.

3.

4.

5.

I will communicate genuinely, assertively, and congruently in the following ways. For example:

1. By not controlling the conversation
2. I will listen to hear.
3. I will take action after thinking things through.

To communicate more assertively, I will do the following:

1.

2.

3.

4.

Note three conflicts you have encountered and offer three solutions to those conflicts.

Conflicts	Solutions
1.	1.
2.	2.
3.	3.

When you are embroiled in a conflict, some of the physiological symptoms you may notice may be: headache, tightness of the muscles in the throat, neck, or shoulders; tightness of the jaw bone; rapid breathing or heart beat; gastrointestinal distress-such as belching, acidic stomach, abdominal cramps, or diarrhea.

Look back to a time when you were engaged in a conflict, What are some behaviors you experienced, that indicates to you now, that there was conflict between you and another person?

How does your body react when you are in conflict with another person? List your bodily reactions below:

Example: I am aware that I tighten my shoulders during a verbal altercation with another person.

1.

2.

3.

4.

Some of the things I can/will do to lessen or prevent conflict with others are:

Coping mechanism I can employ to manage stress or prevent conflict is: Example - become aware of my illogical or irrational thought patterns.

Affirmations To Heal The Person

Today I remember: Worry is like a rocking chair. It will give me something to do, but it won't get me anywhere.

Life is full of ends, but every end is a new beginning.

As Charlie Chester says on the BBC: "Do good in the world and you might find it doing you a world of good.

Dolly Sewell, Nottingham, England

COMMUNICATION QUOTIENT

Things I do In My Negotiations With Others…
Place a check mark under the appropriate category.

None Seldom Frequent

1. I set limits by saying, no.
2. Soften my tone of voice, or position, so I do not offend.
3. I frequently defend my statements.
4. Tag questions end of my statement.
5. I am too polite, and often do not speak on my behalf.
6. Interrupt others frequently, when they speak.
7. I edit my words, listen, then respond.
8. I know how to block interruptions.

Check the lines above and write the words none, seldom or frequent to indicate how often you do the above. Give yourself a plus three if you answered frequently to # 1,2,7,8 and plus two if you answered seldom to # 1,2,7,8. If you answered frequently to # 4,5,6, give yourself a minus three and if you answered none to # 3,4,5,6 give yourself a plus three. Give yourself a plus two if you answered seldom to # 6, and a minus two if you answered seldom to # 5.

If your minus scores cancel out your plus scores, you are doing great. If not, you need to work more on developing your soft power skills.

THE CRITERIA REQUIRED TO CREATE CHANGE IN YOUR NEGOTIATIONS STYLE

Our negotiation style is as natural to us as is the way we walk or talk. By now, we have learned a pattern of behaviors, to get us the things we want in life. The way we behave now is either working or not working for us. But because these behaviors worked earlier for us as children, many of us continue to use them although they be outmoded or ineffective. We only change our behavior if it becomes too painful, or if we are placed in a position where it is to our detriment, to continue in the manner we have in the past.

A change in behavior requires that we give up prior learned behaviors to learn new behaviors we do not know, and which will require effort, time, and practice of us, for the new behavior to feel natural and spontaneous. We must have a strong desire or be highly motivated with an expectation of positive reward to change our negotiation style. Analyze your motive to see if you will be able to persist in changing the way you negotiate with others. The following guidelines will be helpful:

1. Identify the change that is desired.

2. Diagnose your blocks to change the behavior. Identify what the blocks are by asking yourself, what are my blocks?

3. Plan action steps through problem solving techniques, mind mapping or strategic planning

4. Enlist assistance from others through a support group or enroll in a class

5. To initiate change, begin now. Take small action activities that you can do, want to do, and will do. Follow through on what you decide to do. Work on one activity for 1-3 months, so that you can realize a measure of success.

6. Ask for comments from others. Example: Mary, I have been working on being more direct in my communication with

others, have you noticed a change in this area? Even if they say no, realize that minute behavioral changes, may not be recognized by strangers or persons close to you, because they may be afraid that if you change, you may no longer be their friend or acquaintance.

Thought and Words of Wisdom

Watch your thoughts;
they become words.
Watch your words;
They become actions.
Watch your actions;
They become habits.
Watch your character;
It becomes your destiny.

Frank Outlaw

DO YOU HAVE WHAT IT TAKES TO BE A NEGOTIATOR?

When You Resolve Conflict, Do You?
Acknowledge conflict and accept it.

1. Confront it by accepting the role you play to keep it active

2. Avoid conflict due to prior conditioning of fear or expression of anger, due to a need to protect yourself or others? Have an image of yourself as sweet and loving? Have feelings of rebellion?

3. Deny the existence and reality of conflict, so you believe that everything is okay, when it is not.

4. Try to persuade/force others to give you what you want.

5. Accommodate due to prior childhood conditioning of family role models.

6. Collaborate, manipulate or bribe to get your way.

7. Negotiate, compromise from integrity to reach an equitable and fair solution that benefits both you and the other party. Your comments here.

Ida Greene, Ph.D.

DO YOU HAVE POWER?

To Assess Your Power potential, Ask Yourself These Questions:

1. Does my superior, co-worker or significant other care about what I think?

2. Has anyone ever asked my opinion about this or another matter?

3. Am I held in high esteem by my superior/s or coworkers?

4. What power or influence do I have? Is there something I can say or do that will make a difference in the outcome?

5. Should I let my thoughts/ideas be known? Why?

6. Is this issue important to me? Have I invested energy and time in the project/task? Do I care about the outcome?

7. What advantage (power) does the other party have regarding this matter? Situation?

8. What can I do to increase my power base (things I need to know to make my decisions).

9. How can I offset any negative aspects of the way the other person uses power.

10. Do I want responsibility (power)?

11. Can I handle all of the tasks/demands this situation may entail?

12. Am I content to be a watcher or do I want to take the risk to be involved/committed?

How To Better Know Yourself

Know your strengths and weaknesses so that you empower yourself and others. Start by working on your fears. Your fears mask both your strengths and weakness. Your strengths are whatever others praise you on. Your weakness is the things you avoid, because of your fears, be they real or imagined.

Do you know what are your strengths and weakness? List them below.

MY STRENGTHS   MY WEAKNESS

Go over the definitions below, to see how you your definition of yourself matches those given:

POWER IS: Strength, leadership, control of destiny, knowledge, money, and influence. Can you honestly say that you are a powerful person?

POWER IS NOT: Weakness, laziness, cautions behavior, lack of knowledge, or direction. It is the empowerment of one self.

EMPOWERMENT - Power comes from within oneself. It is your behavioral characteristics and style of interacting with others. What can you do today to increase your likelihood of empowering your self?

Chapter 13

USE POSITIVE ASSERTION TO ENHANCE YOUR NEGOTIATION STYLE

Our negotiation style is a composite behavioral characterization of the roles we play in life and a reflection of the many faces we wear. We move in and out of roles through out the day, depending upon the people and circumstances we encounter. This requires flexibility and a willingness to learn about ourselves and others to become a skilled negotiator. It may require that we create a new role, or modify our present manner of interacting to be able to adapt to a new person or situation. Whether we realize or not, we are forever creating. However most of us resort to prior learned behavioral patterns. We do not change our behavior unless we are highly motivated to do so. There has to be a payoff that is to our advantage or perceived by us to be in our best interest.

To understand our style of negotiation, we must be aware of our intentions, values, and our non-verbal communication. Our non verbal communication, often referred to as body language reveals a lot of information about us to another person. Are you aware of your body language? What messages are you sending to others? We send messages to others through our gestures - eye movement, frown on face, tight jaws, pursed lips etc. Though our body movement, we communicate to others, that we are afraid, threatened, hostile, aggressive or friendly.

How well do you know yourself? What unspoken message/s are you sending to others? Are others getting the message you want them to get? Take a moment now and reflect on your body language. Write down how you perceive yourself, then ask an acquaintance to give you feedback about your body language.

Analyzing My Non-Verbal Speech Patterns

Very Often I Hear Myself Saying:

1.

2.

3.

4.

PLAN OF ACTION

In the future to solve this problem I shall:

1.

2.

3.

4.

Beginning Date:_____

Assertive Self-Assessment

1. PASSIVE BEHAVIOR - allows others to invade, take advantage of, and control with your consent.

2. AGGRESSIVE BEHAVIOR - the person invades, controls, and takes advantage of others.

3. PASSIVE/AGGRESSIVE BEHAVIOR - provides a way to manipulate others by indirect, dishonest messages.

4. ASSERTIVE BEHAVIOR - allows one to express thoughts, feelings and beliefs openly, honestly, directly, and appropriately.

BEHAVIORAL STYLES OF RELATING TO OTHERS

Victim/Defeatist
PASSIVE
self-pitying
apologetic
self-punishing
doormat
injured/feels injured
avoids
giving up easily
withdraws
unresponsive
sacrificing
acquiesces
inhibited

unexpressive
limited or no eye contact
retreat
ignore
sweet
cry/cries easily
helpless
anxious
humiliated
insecure
timid
self-denying
martyred

SELF CENTERED	PASSIVE/AGGRESSIVE
Controlled/Dominator	Confused Communication,
(controlled by internal & other external stimuli)	(Double-Messages)
insisting	grudge carrying
dominates	resentful
pushy	spiteful
overbearing	dishonest
overpowering	bitter
violent	gossipy
loud	revengeful
destructive	unaware
hostile	manipulative
superior	gives double messages
bossy	indignant
mean	cynical
thoughtless	inconsistent
threatening	indirect
explosive	phony
right	confusing
ridiculing	sarcastic
contemptuous	sulky
belittling	uneasy
inconsiderate	fearful
preachy	anxious
harsh	late
punishing	insults easily
invading	devious
interrupting	condescending

ASSERTIVE BEHAVIOR
clear
direct
aware
spontaneous
energized
powerful
moving
honest
responsible for self
open
choosing
appropriate
negotiating
listening
confident
centered
expressive
coaxes
flexible
confront
in control of self
considerate
competent
relaxed

Check Your Emotional Health
check the appropriate word/s above that applies to you. Then write how this affects your self-esteem in relation to negotiation or your use of power.

Ida Greene, Ph.D.

Are You a Negotiator? You Decide

Write your answer in the space below:
1. How do you like to problem solve? Alone or in group?

2. How well do you work with others in team work? Do you have skills in this area. Do you need assistance? How pragmatic are you?

3. Are you comfortable in asking for help, when you don't understand? What is the risk for you to not know?

4. What are your ego strengths? (ex) jovial, friendly, objective, open minded?

5. How do you handle situations where the answers is not readily observable?

6. What has been your method to deal with conflict? avoidance, overpower, out maneuver, non-reveal?

7. Do you explain your feelings using "I" statements? Are you shy or timid? Do you have low self-esteem? Do you lack confidence in yourself or negotiation skills?

8. Do you accept/acknowledge the consequences of your decisions? Do you accept responsibility for your behavior/decisions?

9. Are you a bottom-line, no nonsense type of person? Do you refuse to discuss things or tend to see thing in very narrow confines?

10. Are you comfortable enough to ask for what you want? Do you feel you deserve to have your needs met? Why?

Ida Greene, Ph.D.

DEVELOP YOUR PROBLEM SOLVING SKILLS

What Strategies Would You Use to solve This Problems?

You recently bought an article of clothing, 100% cotton. The first time you wear the item, you get a food stain on it. You use a stain remover on it which stains the fabric. You attempt to use a colorfast bleach to remove the dark stains and it takes out the original beautiful turquoise color, and the black stain still remains in the fabric. You call the store where you bought this exquisite item and inform them of the situation and ask them to make some adjustment. They inform you that you should have read the washing instructions, which told you to not use bleach, only soap and water. You feel stupid for not reading the directions, however you are out of $60, you really like the item but it is damaged beyond dyeing and you will have to discard it. What do you do?

Can you creatively negotiate the above issue?
Write out your answer(s).

APPLY the PRINCIPLES OF NEGOTIATION

Personal Assessment

Share a problem you had, or now have. come up with some new options to handle the problem. Write out your answer. Now pair off with someone, read your problem to them, listen to what they have to say, and write down their solution. Now discuss the issues together and come up with the best possible solution.

Write down the strategy you used?

What worked?

What didn't work?

Why?

Do you work better as a team or alone? Write down the advantages of both approaches for you.

Why?

What did you learn about the process of Negotiation? What did you learn about yourself.

POSITIVE WORDS TO LIVE BY

> I release all critical and negative thinking of myself,
> and others. Other people are a mirror of me.
> I accept my perfection and wholeness.
> I breathe in God and I breathe out irritation.
> I breathe in God and I breathe out frustration.
> I breathe in God and breathe out limitation or lack.
> I breathe in wealth, and my whole being responds.
> I am renewed, reinvigorated, restored and vitalized
> I am ready to begin again!

Reread this book several times to update your knowledge about soft power negotiation skills. Begin to notice how others negotiate. Make a careful study of areas, you would like to improve and begin to take corrective action.

There will always be negative factors in our lives which if not controlled will erode the positive beliefs we hold about ourselves. If you are treated with disdain and disrespect often you may come to believe that there is something intrinsically wrong with you. People who feel they are unworthy or undeserving are less likely to negotiate on their behalf or if they do, they may be willing to accept far less than they should.

What Is Your Behavioral Style In Dealing With Problems?

Did you tend to gloss over or evade issues? How comfortable were you with ambiguities and discrepancies? Did you have bodily reactions during the exercise that took your attention away from the task at hand? How did you resolve this?

What additional skills or assistance do you feel you need to be a better negotiator? Would you like a class or personal coaching to practice the information you just learned? If the answer to your question is yes, you can call me, Dr. Ida Greene for personal or professional Coaching at 877-767- LOVE (5683). To purchase other books and tapes, People Skills International, contact us at: www.idagreene.com or by E-mail: idagreene@earthlink.net

Ida Greene, Ph.D.

INDEX

	Page
1. Assertiveness Assessment	111
2. Factors involved in Hard Power	21
3. Five Negotiation Styles	63
4. How to Develop Soft Power Skills	96
5. How to Enhance Your Negotiation Style	91, 92, 102
6. Identify Your Negotiation Style	83, 87, 105
7. Negotiation Guidelines	54
8. Principles of Negotiation	54
9. Process of Negotiation	53
10. Rules of Negotiation	55
11. Soft Power Negotiation Skills	35, 38
12. Soft Power Words	41
13. The Soft Side of Power	17, 42
14. The Steps of Negotiation	58
15. Three Stages of Negotiation	58
16. Why We Negotiate	2, 114

Ida Greene, Ph.D.

BIBLIOGRAPHY

Dawson, Roger. *You Can Get Anything You Want (But You Have To Do More Than Ask)*. New York: Simon and Shuster, 1985.

Kings James Version. *Holy Bible*. New York: Thomas Nelson Publishers, 1984.

McKeachie, Wilbert James and Doyle, Charlotte Lackner, *Psychology*. Reading, Massachusetts: Addison-Wesley Publishing Company, Inc., 1966.

Nirenberg, Gerald. *Fundamentals of Negotiating*. New York: Hawthorn Books, Inc.

Nirenberg, Juliet and Ross, Irene. *Women and the Art of Negotiating*. New York: Simon and Shuster, 1985.

ABOUT THE AUTHOR

We all have an Ignitable fire within us! Dr. Ida Greene help you light it and keep it ablaze. Dr. Greene's philosophy is simple: "If it can be done, I can do it!" Dr. Greene contends, that whatever your mind can CONCEIVE and you truly BELIEVE, you can and will ACHIEVE. She holds a Ph.D. is a Registered Nurse, Hypnotherapist, Licensed Marriage and Family, Child Therapist, Educator and Motivational Speaker. She also is the author of nine books: *Light the Fire Within You, Are You Ready for Success?, Soft Power Negotiation Skills, How to Be A Success In Business, Self-Esteem, the Essence of You, How to Improve Self-Esteem In The African American Child, How to Improve Self-Esteem In Any Child, Money: How to Get It, How to Keep It*, and *Say Goodbye to Your Smallness, Hello to Your Greatness*.

Ida can show you, how to use *Soft Power Negotiating Skills*, to add zest to any relationship. Everyone can use Soft Power Negotiation principles to create instant rapport with others, to improve their communication skills. Everyone wants to be a success.

www.ingramcontent.com/pod-product-compliance
Lightning Source LLC
Chambersburg PA
CBHW031922240526
45464CB00022B/642